Ninja Foodi 2-Basket Air Fryer Cookbook

Easy & Delicious Air Fry, Dehydrate, Roast, Bake, Reheat, and More Recipes for Beginners and Advanced Users

Helen Bently

TABLE OF CONTENTS

Chapter 6-Seafood and Fish Recipes

Chapter 7-Vegetables Recipes 69

Chapter 8-Desserts Recipes 79

Chapter 9-3 Weeks Diet Plan 89

Conclusion 93

Chapter 1- Ninja Foodi 2-Basket Air Fryer

The Ninja Foodi 2-Basket Air Fryer is a new arrival amongst their wide range of air fryers. This air fryer has 2 independent baskets that let you cook two different food items or bulk of food at the same time with two different or the same settings. It is way different than the traditional air fryer that usually has a single basket.

As by the name, this comprehensive guide is targeted toward all those busy people who want to enjoy some delicious but less fatty meal that tastes delicious and its texture is as crispy as restaurant meals.

So, if you are a housewife or have an on-to-go lifestyle, then this Ninja Foodi is an excellent appliance to fulfill all the cooking needed. Whether it an early morning breakfast, afternoon brunch, or late-night dinner party, now you can create some remarkable restaurant-style meals right in your kitchen.

Take advantage of any of the recipes provided in this cookbook to enjoy a meal that keeps your weight maintained.

The ninja Foodi 2 basket air fryer lets you prepare food that is delicious and offers a hand-free cooking experience with less hustle. This cookbook includes easily prepared meals targeted toward the American audience.

No doubt, the Ninja foodie 2-basket air fryer plays a very important role in making healthy meals. Unlike, any other appliance like a deep fryer and broiler it prepares food in less oil. Now, stop sacrificing the taste and texture and enjoy whatever you liked.

In this cookbook we are covering the following:

- Introduction
- The Functions of Ninja Foodi 2-Basket Air Fryer
- How to Use Ninja Foodi 2 Basket Air Fryer
- Maintaining and Cleaning the Appliance
- 80 delicious and mouth warring recipes
- 3-week diet plan
- Conclusion

Along with the 80 recipes, we have added beautiful images of the recipes and snippets of the nutritional information, so that that overall calories intake process stays on right track.

What is Ninja Foodi 2-Basket Air Fryer

The new Ninja 2-basket air fryer has a DUAL-ZONE technology that includes a smart finish button that cooks two food items in two different ways at the same time. It has a MATCH button that cooks food by copying the setting across both zones.

The 8 –quart air fryer has a capacity that can cook full family meals up to 4 pounds. The two zones have their separate baskets that cook food using cyclonic fans that heat food rapidly with circulating hot air all-around. The baskets are very easy to clean and dishwasher safe. The ninja Foodi 2-basket air fryer has a range of 105-450 degrees F temperature.

The Ninja foodie 2-basket air fryer is easily available at an affordable price online and at local stores.

If you are always worried about the lack of time to prepare two different meals or a large number of meals in a single go, then this appliance is a must to have.

It can hold plenty of food that can feed a large family.

The Functions of Ninja Foodi 2-Basket Air Fryer

This Ninja foodie 2-Basket Air fryer eliminates the traditional back-to-back cooking by providing ease of two baskets that cook food at the same time.

Its function includes a Smart Finish feature cooking system, so both items of food are cooked at the same time.

This Ninja foodie air fryer surely makes crispy food by removing the moist from the food by circulating the hot air around.

The Ninja® Air Fryer function includes.

- Air Fry
- Air Broil
- Roast
- Bake
- Reheat
- Dehydrate

Package Dimensions: 18.3 x 16.3 x 15.7 inches

Item Weight: 24.3 pounds

Manufacturer: Ninja

If you want to end the cooking time of one zone, while using both zones you need to choose the zone you like to stop, and then press the START/STOP to end the cooking process for that specific zone.

When the drawer is removed from the Ninja foodie 2-basket air fryer, the cooking process is automatically stopped.

The TEMP arrows are used to set the desired temperature.

The TIME arrows are used to set the time according to specific needs.

Once cooking is done the "END" appears on the screen.

How to Use Ninja Foodi 2 Basket Air Fryer

The use of Ninja foodie 2-basket air fryer is as easy as a click of a button.

For most of the recipes, it is necessary and recommended to grease the air fryer baskets with oil spray.

You simply add the food to the basket and select the required function to AIR FRY, BROIL, BAKE, roast, and more.

The +and – buttons to adjust the cooking time and temperature control button can be separately used to adjust the cooking time of the food in both zones.

Once the food gets cooked, you can take out the baskets and serve food from both zones of the air fryer to the serving plates.

Some useful button to cook food:

MAX CRISP: It is used to prepare some of the crispest French fries and chicken nuggets. With lesser amount of oil, you can make more crispy food than a traditional fryer.

ROAST: The roast function easily prepares some tender and juicy meat in no time.

REHEAT: The reheat function can easily help you enjoy any leftover food.

DEHYDRATE: Now you can easily dehydrate most of the fruits and the vegetables, and save money you spend to buy a separate dehydrator.

BAKE: This function helps creates delicious dessert and baked treats.

SYNC button: This button can be used when the user wants to finish two different zones with different settings together.

MATCH button: This button automatically matches both the zone time and temperature.

STANDBY MODE: The unit remains with no interaction for more than 10 minutes, it goes to standby mode.

HOLD MODE: This will appear during sync mode, as one zone is cooking and the other is on hold.

Temperature Ranges

- Bake Function:250- 400 Degrees F (Up To 1-1/2 Hour)
- Roast Function: 250-400 Degrees F (For Up To 4 Hours)
- Reheat Fucniton:270 Degrees F To 400degrees F (1minutes to 1hours)
- Dehydrate Functions: 105 -195 Degrees F (1-12 Hours)
- Air Broil Function400 Degrees F To 450 Degrees F (1 Minutes 30 Minutes)

Maintaining and Cleaning the Appliance

- The Ninja 2-basket air fryer is not intended to be used outdoor.
- It is very important to check the voltage indication are corresponding to the main voltage from the switch.
- Do not immerse the appliance in water.
- Keep the cord away from the hot area.
- Do not touch the outer surface of the air fryer hen using for cooking purposes.
- Put the appliance on a horizontal and flat surface.
- Unplug the appliance after use.

Cleaning

- First, unplug the power cord of the air fryer.
- Make sure the appliance is cooled before cleaning.
- The air fryer should be cleaning after every use.
- To clean the outer surface, use a damp towel.
- Clean the inside of the air fryer with a nonabrasive sponge.
- The accessories of the air fryer are dishwasher safe, but to extend the life of the drawers, it's recommended to wash them manually.

Chapter 2-Breakfast Recipes

Breakfast Sausage Omelet

Prep: 10 Minutes | Cook Time: 8 Minutes | Makes: 2 Servings

Ingredients

- ¼ pound breakfast sausage, cooked and crumbled
- 4 eggs, beaten
- ½ cup pepper Jack cheese blend
- 2 tablespoons green bell pepper, sliced
- 1 green onion, chopped
- 1 pinch cayenne pepper
- Cooking spray

Directions

1. Take a bowl and whisk eggs in it along with crumbled sausage, pepper Jack cheese, green onions, red bell pepper, and cayenne pepper.
2. Mix it all well.
3. Take two cake pans that fit inside the air fryer and grease it with oil spray.
4. Divide the omelet mixture between cake pans.
5. Put the cake pans inside both of the Ninja Foodie 2-Basket Air Fryer baskets.
6. Turn on the BAKE function of the zone 1 basket and let it cook for 15-20 minutes at 310 degrees F.
7. Select MATCH button for zone 2 basket.
8. Once the cooking cycle completes, take out, and serve hot, as a delicious breakfast.

Serving Suggestion: Serve it with ketchup

Variation Tip: Use Parmesan cheese instead of pepper jack Cheese

Nutritional Information Per Serving: Calories 691| Fat52.4g | Sodium1122 mg | Carbs 13.3g | Fiber 1.8g| Sugar 7g | Protein 42g

Sausage with Eggs

Prep: 10 Minutes | Cook Time: 13 Minutes | Makes: 2 Servings

Ingredients

- 4 sausage links, raw and uncooked
- 4 eggs, uncooked
- 1 tablespoon of green onion
- 2 tablespoons of chopped tomatoes
- Salt and black pepper, to taste
- 2 tablespoons of milk, dairy
- Oil spray, for greasing

Directions

1. Take a bowl and whisk eggs in it.
2. Then pour milk, and add onions and tomatoes.
3. Whisk it all well.
4. Now season it with salt and black pepper.
5. Take one cake pan, that fit inside the air fryer and grease it with oil spray.
6. Pour the omelet in the greased cake pans.
7. Put the cake pan inside zone 1 air fryer basket of Ninja Foodie 2-Basket Air Fryer.
8. Now place the sausage link into the zone 2 basket.
9. Select bake for zone 1 basket and set the timer to 8-10 minutes at 300 degrees F.
10. For the zone 2 basket, select the AIR FRY button and set the timer to 12 minutes at 390 degrees.
11. Once the cooking cycle completes, serve by transferring it to plates.
12. Chop the sausage or cut it in round and then mix it with omelet.
13. Enjoy hot as a delicious breakfast.

Serving Suggestion: Serve it with toasted bread slices

Variation Tip: Use almond milk if like non-dairy milk

Nutritional Information Per Serving: Calories 240 | Fat 18.4g| Sodium 396mg | Carbs 2.8g | Fiber0.2g | Sugar 2g | Protein 15.6g

reakfast Casserole

Prep: 5 Minutes | Cook Time: 10 Minutes | Makes: 4 Servings

Ingredients

- 1 pound of beef sausage, grounded
- 1/4 cup diced white onion
- 1 diced green bell pepper
- 8 whole eggs, beaten
- ½ cup Colby jack cheese, shredded
- ¼ teaspoon of garlic salt
- Oil spray, for greasing

Directions

1. Take a bowl and add ground sausage to it.
2. Add in the diced onions, bell peppers, eggs and whisk it well.
3. Then season it with garlic salt.
4. Spray both the baskets of the air fryer with oil spray.
5. Divide this mixture among the baskets; remember to remove the crisper plates.
6. Top the mixture with cheese.
7. Now, turn ON the Ninja Foodie 2-Basket Air Fryer zone 1 and select AIR FRY mode and set the time to 10 minutes at 390 degrees F.
8. Select the MATCH button for zone 2 baskets, and hit start.
9. Once the cooking cycle completes, take out, and serve.
10. Serve and enjoy.

Serving Suggestion: Serve it with sour cream

Variation Tip: Use turkey sausages instead of beef sausages.

Nutritional Information Per Serving: Calories 699| Fat 59.1g | Sodium 1217 mg | Carbs 6.8g | Fiber 0.6g| Sugar 2.5g | Protein33.1 g

Bacon and Eggs for Breakfast

Prep: 12 Minutes | Cook Time: 12 Minutes | Makes: 1 Serving

Ingredients

- 4 strips of thick-sliced bacon
- 2 small eggs
- Salt and black pepper, to taste
- Oil spray for greasing ramekins

Directions

1. Take 2 ramekins and grease them with oil spray.
2. Crack eggs in a bowl and season it salt and black pepper.
3. Divide the egg mixture between two ramekins.
4. Put the bacon slices into Ninja Foodie 2-Basket Air Fryer zone 1 basket, and ramekins in zone 2 baskets.
5. Now for zone 1 set it to AIR FRY mode at 400 degrees F for 12 minutes.
6. And for zone 2 set it 350 degrees for 8 minutes using AIR FRY mode.
7. Press the Smart finish button and press start, it will finish both at the same time.
8. Once done, serve and enjoy.

Serving Suggestion: None

Variation Tip: Use butter for greasing ramekins

Nutritional Information Per Serving: Calories131 | Fat 10g| Sodium 187mg | Carbs0.6 g | Fiber 0g | Sugar 0.6g | Protein 10.7

Bacon and Egg Omelet

Prep: 12 Minutes | Cook Time: 10 Minutes | Makes: 2 Servings

Ingredients

- 2 eggs, whisked
- ½ teaspoon of chopped tomatoes
- Sea Salt and black pepper, to taste
- 2 teaspoons of almond milk
- 1 teaspoon of cilantro, chopped
- 1 small green chili, chopped
- 4 slices of bacon

Directions

1. Take a bowl and whisk eggs in it.
2. Then add green chili salt, black pepper, cilantro, almond milk, and chopped tomatoes.
3. Oil greases the ramekins.
4. Pour this into ramekins.
5. Put the bacon in the zone 1 basket and ramekins in zone 2 basket of the Ninja Foodie 2-Basket Air Fryer.
6. Now for zone 1, set it to AIR FRY mode at 400 degrees F for 10 minutes
7. And for zone 2, set it 350 degrees for 10 minutes in AIR FRY mode.
8. Press the Smart finish button and press start, it will finish both at the same time.
9. Once done, serve and enjoy.

Serving Suggestion: Serve it with bread slices and ketchup

Variation Tip: Use garlic salt instead of sea salt

Nutritional Information Per Serving: Calories 285| Fat 21.5g| Sodium1000 mg | Carbs 2.2g | Fiber 0.1g| Sugar1 g | Protein 19.7g

Egg and Avocado in The Ninja Foodi

Prep: 10 Minutes | Cook Time: 12 Minutes | Makes: 2 Servings

Ingredients

- 2 Avocados, pitted and cut in half
- Garlic salt, to taste
- Cooking for greasing
- 4 eggs
- ¼ teaspoon of Paprika powder, for sprinkling
- 1/3 cup parmesan cheese, crumbled
- 6 bacon strips, raw

Directions

1. First cut the avocado in half and pit it.
2. Now scoop out the flesh from the avocado and keep intact some of it
3. Crack one egg in each hole of avocado and sprinkle paprika and garlic salt
4. Top it with cheese at the end.
5. Now put it into tin foils and then put it in the air fryer zone basket 1
6. Put bacon strips in zone 2 basket.
7. Now for zone 1, set it to AIR FRY mode at 350 degrees F for 10 minutes
8. And for zone 2, set it 400 degrees for 12 minutes AIR FRY mode.
9. Press the Smart finish button and press start, it will finish both at the same time.
10. Once done, serve and enjoy.

Serving Suggestion: Serve it with Bread slices

Variation Tip: Use butter for greasing

Nutritional Information Per Serving: Calories609 | Fat53.2g | Sodium 335mg | Carbs 18.1g | Fiber13.5g | Sugar 1.7g | Protein 21.3g

Yellow Potatoes with Eggs

Prep: 10 Minutes | Cook Time: 35 Minutes | Makes: 2 Servings

Ingredients

- 1 pound of Dutch yellow potatoes, quartered
- 1 red bell pepper, chopped
- Salt and black pepper, to taste
- 1 green bell pepper, chopped
- 2 teaspoons of olive oil
- 2 teaspoons of garlic powder
- 1 teaspoon of onion powder
- 1 egg
- ¼ teaspoon of butter

Directions

1. Toss together diced potatoes, green pepper, red pepper, salt, black pepper, and olive oil along with garlic powder and onion powder.
2. Put in the zone 1 basket of the air fryer.
3. Take ramekin and grease it with oil spray.
4. Whisk egg in a bowl and add salt and pepper along with ½ teaspoon of butter.
5. Pour egg into a ramekin and place it in a zone 2 basket.
6. Now start cooking and set a timer for zone 1 basket to 30-35 minutes at 400 degrees at AIR FRY mode.
7. Now for zone 2, set it on AIR FRY mode at 350 degrees F for 8-10 minutes.
8. Press the Smart finish button and press start, it will finish both at the same time.
9. Once done, serve and enjoy.

Serving Suggestion: Serve it with sourdough toasted bread slices

Variation Tip: Use white potatoes instead of yellow Dutch potatoes.

Nutritional Information Per Serving: Calories252 | Fat7.5g | Sodium 37mg | Carbs 40g | Fiber3.9g | Sugar 7g | Protein 6.7g

Sweet Potatoes Hash

Prep: 15 Minutes | Cook Time: 25 Minutes | Makes: 2 Servings

Ingredients

- 450 grams sweet potatoes
- 1/2 white onion, diced
- 3 tablespoons of olive oil
- 1 teaspoon smoked paprika
- 1/4 teaspoon cumin
- 1/3 teaspoon of ground turmeric
- 1/4 teaspoon of garlic salt
- 1 cup guacamole

Directions

1. Peel and cut the potatoes into cubes.
2. Now, transfer the potatoes to a bowl and add oil, white onions, cumin, paprika, turmeric, and garlic salt.
3. Put this mixture between both the baskets of the Ninja Foodie 2-Basket Air Fryer.
4. Set it to AIR FRY mode for 10 minutes at 390 degrees F.
5. Then take out the baskets and shake them well.
6. Then again set time to 15 minutes at 390 degrees F.
7. Once done, serve it with guacamole.

Serving Suggestion: serve it with ketchup and omelet

Variation Tip: Use canola oil instead of olive oil

Nutritional Information Per Serving: Calories691 | Fat 49.7g| Sodium 596mg | Carbs 64g | Fiber15g | Sugar 19g | Protein 8.1g

Egg with Baby Spinach

Prep: 12 Minutes | Cook Time: 12 Minutes | Makes: 4 Servings

Ingredients

- Nonstick spray, for greasing ramekins
- 2 tablespoons olive oil
- 6 ounces baby spinach
- 2 garlic cloves, minced
- 1/3 teaspoon kosher salt
- 6-8 large eggs
- ½ cup half and half
- Salt and black pepper, to taste
- 8 Sourdough bread slices, toasted

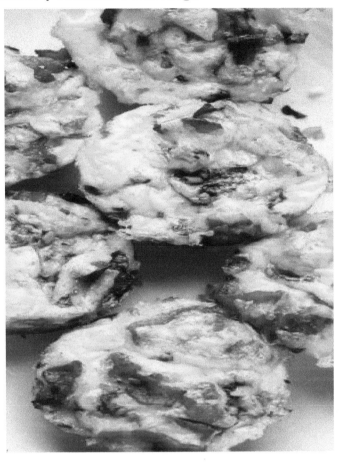

Directions

1. Grease 4 ramekins with oil spray and set aside for further use.
2. Take a skillet and heat oil in it.
3. Then cook spinach for 2 minutes and add garlic and salt black pepper.
4. Let it simmer for2more minutes.
5. Once the spinach is wilted, transfer it to a plate.
6. Whisk an egg into a small bowl.
7. Add in the spinach.
8. Whisk it well and then pour half and half.
9. Divide this mixture between 4 ramekins and remember not to overfill it to the top, leave a little space on top.
10. Put the ramekins in zone 1 and zone 2 baskets of the Ninja Foodie 2-Basket Air Fryer.
11. Press start and set zone 1 to AIR fry it at 350 degrees F for 8-12 minutes.
12. Press the MATCH button for zone 2.
13. Once it's cooked and eggs are done, serve with sourdough bread slices.

Serving Suggestion: Serve it with cream cheese topping

Variation Tip: Use plain bread slices instead of sourdough bread slices.

Nutritional Information Per Serving: Calories 404| Fat 19.6g| Sodium 761mg | Carbs 40.1g | Fiber 2.5g| Sugar 2.5g | Protein 19.2g

Banana and Raisins Muffins

Prep: 20 Minutes | Cook Time: 16 Minutes | Makes: 2 Servings

Ingredients

- Salt, pinch
- 2 eggs, whisked
- 1/3 cup butter, melted
- 4 tablespoons of almond milk
- ¼ teaspoon of vanilla extract
- ½ teaspoon of baking powder
- 1-1/2 cup all-purpose flour
- 1 cup mashed bananas
- 2 tablespoons of raisins

Directions

1. Take about 4 large (one-cup sized) ramekins and layer them with muffin papers.
2. Crack eggs in a large bowl, and whisk it all well and start adding vanilla extract, almond milk, baking powder, and melted butter
3. Whisk the ingredients very well.
4. Take a separate bowl and add the all-purpose flour, and salt.
5. Now, combine the add dry ingredients with the wet ingredients.
6. Now, pour mashed bananas and raisins into this batter
7. Mix it well to make a batter for the muffins.
8. Now pour the batter into four ramekins and divided the ramekins in the air fryer zones.
9. Set the timer for zone 1 to 16 minutes at 350 degrees F.
10. Select the MATCH button for the zone 2 basket.
11. Check if not done, and let it AIR FRY for one more minute.
12. Once it is done, serve.

Serving Suggestion: None

Variation Tip: None

Nutritional Information Per Serving: Calories 727| Fat 43.1g| Sodium366 mg | Carbs 74.4g | Fiber 4.7g | Sugar 16.1g | Protein 14.1g

Chapter 3-Snacks and Appetizers Recipes

Blueberries Muffins

Prep: 15 Minutes | Cook Time: 15 Minutes | Makes: 2 Servings

Ingredients

- Salt, pinch
- 2 eggs
- 1/3 cup sugar
- 1/3 cup vegetable oil
- 4 tablespoons of water
- 1 teaspoon of lemon zest
- ¼ teaspoon of vanilla extract
- ½ teaspoon of baking powder
- 1 cup all-purpose flour
- 1 cup blueberries

Directions

1. Take 4 one-cup sized ramekins that are oven safe and layer them with muffin papers.
2. Take a bowl and whisk the egg, sugar, oil, water, vanilla extract, and lemon zest.
3. Whisk it all very well.
4. Now, in a separate bowl, mix the flour, baking powder, and salt.
5. Now, add dry ingredients slowly to wet ingredients.
6. Now, pour this batter into ramekins and top it with blueberries.

7. Now, divide it between both zones of the Ninja Foodie 2-Basket Air Fryer.
8. Set the time for zone 1 to 15 minutes at 350 degrees F.
9. Select the MATCH button for the zone 2 basket.
10. Check if not done, and let it AIR FRY for one more minute.
11. Once it is done, serve.

Serving Suggestion: Serve it with whipped cream topping

Variation Tip: use butter instead of vegetable oil

Nutritional Information Per Serving: Calories 781| Fat41.6g | Sodium 143mg | Carbs 92.7g | Fiber 3.5g| Sugar41.2 g | Protein 0g

Cheddar Quiche

Prep: 10 Minutes | Cook Time: 12 Minutes | Makes: 2 Servings

Ingredients

- 4 eggs, organic
- 1-1/4 cup heavy cream
- Salt, pinch
- ½ cup broccoli florets
- ½ cup cheddar cheese, shredded and for sprinkling

Directions

1. Take a Pyrex pitcher and crack two eggs in it.
2. And fill it with heavy cream, about half the way up.
3. Add in the salt and then add in the broccoli and pour this into two quiche dishes, and top it with shredded cheddar cheese.
4. Now divide it between both zones of baskets.
5. For zone 1, set the time to 10-12 minutes at 325 degrees F.
6. Select the MATCH button for the zone 2 basket.
7. Once done, serve hot.

Serving Suggestion: Serve with herbs as a topping

Variation Tip: Use spinach instead of broccoli florets

Nutritional Information Per Serving: Calories 454| Fat40g | Sodium 406mg | Carbs 4.2g | Fiber 0.6g| Sugar1.3 g | Protein 20g

Grill Cheese Sandwich

Prep: 15 Minutes | Cook Time: 10 Minutes | Makes: 2 Servings

Ingredients

- 4 slices of white bread slices
- 2 tablespoons of butter, melted
- 2 slices of sharp cheddar
- 2 slices of Swiss cheese
- 2 slices of mozzarella cheese

Directions

1. Brush melted butter on one side of all the bread slices and then top the 2 bread slices with slices of cheddar, Swiss, and mozzarella, one slice per bread.

2. Top it with the other slice to make a sandwich.

3. Divide it between two baskets of the air fryer.

4. Turn on AIR FRY mode for zone 1 basket at 350 degrees F for 10 minutes.

5. Use the MATCH button for the second zone.

6. Once done, serve.

Serving Suggestion: Serve with tomato soup

Variation Tip: Use oil spray instead of butter

Nutritional Information Per Serving: Calories 577 | Fat38g | Sodium 1466mg | Carbs 30.5g | Fiber 1.1g| Sugar 6.5g | Protein 27.6g

Dijon Cheese Sandwich

Prep: 10 Minutes | Cook Time: 10 Minutes | Makes: 2 Servings

Ingredients

- 4 large slices sourdough, whole grain
- 4 tablespoons of Dijon mustard
- 1-1/2 cup grated sharp cheddar cheese
- 2 teaspoons green onion, chopped the green part
- 2 tablespoons of butter melted

Directions

1. Brush the melted butter on one side of all the bread slices.
2. Then spread Dijon mustard on other sides of slices.
3. Then top the 2 bread slices with cheddar cheese and top it with green onions.
4. Cover with the remaining two slices to make two sandwiches.
5. Divide it between two baskets of the air fryer.
6. Turn on the air fry mode for zone 1 basket at 350 degrees f, for 10 minutes.
7. Use the match button for the second zone.
8. Once it's done, serve.

Serving Suggestion: Serve with tomato soup

Variation Tip: Use oil spray instead of butter

Nutritional Information Per Serving: calories 617| fat 38 g| sodium 1213mg | carbs40.8 g | fiber 5g| sugar 5.6g | protein 29.5g

Sweet Bites

Prep: 25 Minutes | Cook Time: 12 Minutes | Makes: 4 Servings

Ingredients

- 10 sheets of Phyllo dough, (filo dough)
- 2 tablespoons of melted butter
- 1 cup walnuts, chopped
- 2 teaspoons of honey
- Pinch of cinnamon
- 1 teaspoon of orange zest

Directions

1. First, layer together 10 Phyllo dough sheets on a flat surface.
2. Then cut it into 4 *4-inch squares.
3. Now, coat the squares with butter, drizzle some honey, orange zest, walnuts, and cinnamon.
4. Bring all 4 corners together and press the corners to make a little like purse design.
5. Divide it amongst air fryer basket and select zone 1 basket using AIR fry mode and set it for 7 minutes at 375 degrees F.
6. Select the MATCH button for the zone 2 basket.
7. Once done, take out and serve.

Serving Suggestion: Serve with a topping of nuts

Variation Tip: None

Nutritional Information Per Serving: Calories 397| Fat 27.1 g| Sodium 271mg | Carbs31.2 g | Fiber 3.2g| Sugar3.3g | Protein 11g

Strawberries and Walnuts Muffins

Prep: 15 Minutes | Cook Time: 15 Minutes | Makes: 2 Servings

Ingredients

- Salt, pinch
- 2 eggs, whisked
- 1/3 cup maple syrup
- 1/3 cup coconut oil
- 4 tablespoons of water
- 1 teaspoon of orange zest
- ¼ teaspoon of vanilla extract
- ½ teaspoon of baking powder
- 1 cup all-purpose flour
- 1 cup strawberries, finely chopped
- 1/3 cup walnuts, chopped and roasted

Directions

1. Take one cup size of 4 ramekins that are oven safe.
2. Layer it with muffin paper.
3. In a bowl and add egg, maple syrup, oil, water, vanilla extract, and orange zest.
4. Whisk it all very well
5. In a separate bowl, mix flour, baking powder, and salt.
6. Now add dry ingredients slowly to wet ingredients.
7. Now pour this batter into ramekins and top it with strawberries and walnuts.
8. Now divide it between both zones and set the time for zone 1 basket to 15 minutes at 350 degrees F.
9. Select the MATCH button for the zone 2 basket.
10. Check if not done let it AIR FRY FOR one more minute.
11. Once done, serve.

Serving Suggestion: serve it with coffee

Variation Tip: use vegetable oil instead of coconut oil

Nutritional Information Per Serving: Calories 897| Fat 53.9g | Sodium 148mg | Carbs 92g | Fiber 4.7g| Sugar35.6 g | Protein 17.5g

Chicken Tenders

Prep: 15 Minutes | Cook Time: 12 Minutes | Makes: 3 Servings

Ingredients

- 1 pound of chicken tender
- Salt and black pepper, to taste
- 1 cup Panko bread crumbs
- 2 cups Italian bread crumbs
- 1 cup parmesan cheese
- 2 eggs
- Oil spray, for greasing

Directions

1. Sprinkle the tenders with salt and black pepper.
2. In a medium bowl mix Panko bread crumbs with Italian breadcrumbs.
3. Add salt, pepper, and parmesan cheese.
4. Crack two eggs in a bowl.
5. First, put the chicken tender in eggs.
6. Now dredge the tender in a bowl and coat the tender well with crumbs.
7. Line both of the baskets of the air fryer with parchment paper.
8. At the end spray the tenders with oil spray.
9. Divided the tenders between the baskets of Ninja Foodie 2-Basket Air Fryer.
10. Set zone 1 basket to AIR FRY mode at 350 degrees F for 12 minutes.
11. Select the MATCH button for the zone 2 basket.
12. Once it's done, serve.

Serving Suggestion: Serve it with ranch or ketchup

Variation Tip: Use Italian seasoning instead of Italian bread crumbs

Nutritional Information Per Serving: Calories558 | Fat23.8g | Sodium872 mg | Carbs 20.9g | Fiber1.7 g| Sugar2.2 g | Protein 63.5g

Spicy Chicken Tenders

Prep: 15 Minutes | Cook Time: 12 Minutes | Makes: 2 Servings

Ingredients

- 2 large eggs, whisked
- 2 tablespoons lemon juice
- Salt and black pepper
- 1 pound of chicken tenders
- 1 cup Panko breadcrumbs
- 1/2 cup Italian bread crumb
- 1 teaspoon smoked paprika
- 1/4 teaspoon garlic powder
- 1/4 teaspoon onion powder
- 1/2 cup fresh grated parmesan cheese

Directions

1. Take a bowl and whisk eggs in it and set aside for further use.
2. In a large bowl add lemon juice, paprika, salt, black pepper, garlic powder, onion powder
3. In a separate bowl mix Panko breadcrumbs, Italian bread crumbs, and parmesan cheese.
4. Dip the chicken tender in the spice mixture and coat the entire tender well.
5. Let the tenders sit for 1 hour.
6. Then dip each chicken tender in egg and then in bread crumbs.
7. Line both the basket of the air fryer with parchment paper.
8. Divide the tenders between the baskets.
9. Set zone 1 basket to air fry mode at 350 degrees F for 12 minutes.
10. Select the MATCH button for the zone 2 basket.
11. Once it's done, serve.

Serving Suggestion: Serve it with ketchup

Variation Tip: Use mild paprika instead of smoked paprika

Nutritional Information Per Serving: Calories 836| Fat 36g| Sodium1307 mg | Carbs 31.3g | Fiber 2.5g| Sugar3.3 g | Protein 95.3g

Stuffed Bell Peppers

Prep: 25 Minutes | Cook Time: 16 Minutes | Makes: 3 Servings

Ingredients

- 6 large bell peppers
- 1-1/2 cup cooked rice
- 2 cups cheddar cheese

Directions

1. Cut the bell peppers in half lengthwise and remove all the seeds.
2. Fill the cavity of each bell pepper with cooked rice.
3. Divide the bell peppers amongst the two zones of the air fryer basket.
4. Set the time for zone 1 for 200 degrees for 10 minutes.
5. Select MATCH button of zone 2 basket.
6. Afterward, take out the baskets and sprinkle cheese on top.
7. Set the time for zone 1 for 200 degrees for 6 minutes.
8. Select MATCH button of zone 2 basket.
9. Once it's done, serve.

Serving Suggestion: Serve it with mashed potato

Variation Tip: You can use any cheese you like

Nutritional Information Per Serving: Calories 605| Fat 26g | Sodium477 mg | Carbs68.3 g | Fiber4 g| Sugar 12.5g | Protein25.6 g

Parmesan Crush Chicken

Prep: 20 Minutes | Cook Time: 18 Minutes | Makes: 4 Servings

Ingredients

- 4 chicken breasts
- 1 cup parmesan cheese
- 1 cup bread crumb
- 2 eggs, whisked
- Salt, to taste
- Oil spray, for greasing

Directions

1. Whisk egg in a large bowl and set aside.
2. Season the chicken breast with salt and then put it in egg wash.
3. Next, dredge it in breadcrumb then parmesan cheese.
4. Line both the basket of the air fryer with parchment paper.
5. Divided the breast pieces between the backsets, and oil spray the breast pieces.
6. Set zone 1 basket to air fry mode at 350 degrees F for 18 minutes.
7. Select the MATCH button for the zone 2 basket.
8. Once it's done, serve.

Serving Suggestion: Serve it with ketchup

Variation Tip: Use cheddar cheese instead of parmesan

Nutritional Information Per Serving: Calories574 | Fat25g | Sodium848 mg | Carbs 21.4g | Fiber 1.2g| Sugar 1.8g | Protein 64.4g

Chapter 4-Beef, Lamb and Pork Recipes

Beef & Broccoli

Prep: 12 Minutes | Cook Time: 12 Minutes | Makes: 4 Servings

Ingredients

- 12 ounces of teriyaki sauce, divided
- ½ tablespoon garlic powder
- ¼ cup of soy sauce
- 1 pound raw sirloin steak, thinly sliced
- 2 cups broccoli, cut into florets
- 2 teaspoons of olive oil
- Salt and black pepper, to taste

Directions

1. Take a zip-lock plastic bag and mix teriyaki sauce, salt, garlic powder, black pepper, soy sauce, and olive oil.
2. Marinate the beef in it for 2 hours.
3. Then drain the beef from the marinade.
4. Now toss the broccoli with oil, teriyaki sauce, and salt and black pepper.
5. Put it in a zone 1 basket
6. Now for the zone, 1 basket set it to AIRFRY mode at 400 degrees F for 15 minutes.

7. Place the steak in a zone 2 basket and set it to AIR FRY mode at 375 degrees F for 10-12 minutes.
8. Hit start and let the cooking cycle completes.
9. Once it's done take out the beef and broccoli and
10. serve immediately with leftover teriyaki sauce and cooked rice.

Serving Suggestion: Serve it with mashed potatoes

Variation Tip: Use canola oil instead of olive oil

Nutritional Information Per Serving: Calories 344| Fat 10g| Sodium 4285mg | Carbs18.2 g | Fiber 1.5g| Sugar 13.3g | Protein42 g

Steak and Mashed Creamy Potatoes

Prep: 15 Minutes | Cook Time: 45 Minutes | Makes: 1 Serving

Ingredients

- 2 Russet potatoes, peeled and cubed
- ¼ cup butter, divided
- 1/3 cup heavy cream
- ½ cup shredded cheddar cheese
- Salt and black pepper, to taste
- 1 New York strip steak, about a pound
- 1 teaspoon of olive oil
- Oil spray, for greasing

Directions

1. Rub the potatoes with salt and a little amount of olive oil about a teaspoon.
2. Next, season the steak with salt and black pepper.
3. Place the russet potatoes in a zone 1 basket.
4. Oil spray the steak from both sides and then place it in the zone 2 basket.
5. Set zone 1 to AIR fry mode for 45 minutes at 390 degrees F.
6. Set the zone 2 basket, at 12 minutes at 375 degrees F.
7. Hot start and Lethe ninja foodie do its magic.
8. One the cooking cycle completes, take out the steak and potatoes.
9. Mash the potatoes and then add butter, heavy cream, and cheese along with salt and black pepper.
10. Serve the mashed potatoes with steak.
11. Enjoy.

Serving Suggestion: Serve it with rice

Variation Tip: Use Parmesan instead of cheddar

Nutritional Information Per Serving: Calories1932 | Fat 85.2g| Sodium 3069mg | Carbs 82g | Fiber10.3 g| Sugar 5.3g | Protein 22.5g

Short Ribs & Root Vegetables

Prep: 15 Minutes | Cook Time: 45 Minutes | Makes: 2 Servings

Ingredients

- 1 pound of beef short ribs, bone-in and trimmed
- Salt and black pepper, to taste
- 2 tablespoons canola oil, divided
- 1/4 cup red wine
- 3 tablespoons brown sugar
- 2 cloves garlic, peeled, minced
- 4 carrots, peeled, cut into 1-inch pieces
- 2 parsnips, peeled, cut into 1-inch pieces
- ½ cup pearl onions

Directions

1. Season the ribs with salt and black pepper and rub a little amount of canola oil on both sides.
2. Place it in zone 1 basket of the air fryer.
3. Next, take a bowl and add pearl onions, parsnip, carrots, garlic, brown sugar, red wine, salt, and black pepper.
4. Add the vegetable mixture to the zone 2 basket.
5. Set the zone 1 basket time to 12 minutes at 375 degrees F at AIR FRY mode.
6. Set the zone 2 basket at AIR FRY mode at 390 degrees F for 18 minutes.
7. Hit start so the cooking cycle being.
8. Once the cooking complete, take out the ingredient and serve short ribs with the mixed vegetables and liquid collect at the bottom of zone 2 basket
9. Enjoy it hot.

Serving Suggestion: Serve it with mashed potatoes.

Variation Tip: Use olive oil instead of canola oil.

Nutritional Information Per Serving: Calories1262 | Fat 98.6g| Sodium 595mg | Carbs 57g | Fiber 10.1g| Sugar 28.2g | Protein 35.8g

Steak in Air Fry

Prep: 15 Minutes | Cook Time: 20 Minutes | Makes: 1 Serving

Ingredients

- 2 teaspoons of canola oil
- 1 tablespoon of Montreal steaks seasoning
- 1 pound of beef steak

Directions

1. The first step is to season the steak on both sides with canola oil and then rub a generous amount of steak seasoning all over.
2. We are using the AIR BROIL feature of the ninja air fryer and it works with one basket.
3. Put the steak in the basket and set it to AIR BROIL at 450 degrees F for 20 -22 minutes.
4. After 7 minutes, hit pause and take out the basket to flip the steak, and cover it with foil on top, for the remaining 14 minutes.
5. Once done, serve the medium-rare steak and enjoy it by resting for 10 minutes.
6. Serve by cutting in slices.
7. Enjoy.

Serving Suggestion: Serve it with mashed potatoes

Variation Tip: Use vegetable oil instead of canola oil.

Nutritional Information Per Serving: Calories 935| Fat 37.2g| Sodium 1419mg | Carbs 0g | Fiber 0g| Sugar 0g | Protein137.5 g

Glazed Steak Recipe

Prep: 15 Minutes | Cook Time: 25 Minutes | Makes: 2 Servings

Ingredients

- 1 pound of beef steaks
- ½ cup, soy sauce
- Salt and black pepper, to taste
- 1 tablespoon of vegetable oil
- 1 teaspoon of grated ginger
- 4 cloves garlic, minced
- 1/4 cup brown sugar

Directions

1. Take a bowl and whisk together soy sauce, salt, pepper, vegetable oil, garlic, brown sugar, and ginger.
2. Once a paste is made rub the steak with the marinate
3. Let it sit for 30 minutes.
4. After 30 minutes add the steak to the air fryer basket and set it to AIR BROIL mode at 400 degrees F for 18-22 minutes.
5. After 10 minutes, hit pause and takeout the basket.
6. Let the steak flip and again let it AIR BROIL for the remaining minutes.
7. Once 25 minutes of cooking cycle completes.
8. Take out the steak and let it rest. Serve by cutting into slices.
9. Enjoy.

Serving Suggestion: Serve it with mashed potatoes

Variation Tip: Use canola oil instead of vegetable oil

Nutritional Information Per Serving: Calories 563| Fat 21 g| Sodium 156mg | Carbs 20.6g | Fiber0.3 g| Sugar17.8 g | Protein69.4 g

Chinese BBQ Pork

Prep: 15 Minutes | Cook Time: 25-35 Minutes | Makes: 2 Servings

Sauce Ingredients

- 4 tablespoons of soy sauce
- ¼ cup red wine
- 2 tablespoons of oyster sauce
- ¼ tablespoons of hoisin sauce
- ¼ cup honey
- ¼ cup brown sugar
- Pinch of salt
- Pinch of black pepper
- 1 teaspoon of ginger garlic, paste
- 1 teaspoon of five-spice powder

Other Ingredients

- 1.5 pounds of pork shoulder, sliced

Directions

1. Take a bowl and mix all the ingredients listed under sauce ingredients.
2. Transfer half of it to a sauce pan and let it cook for 10 minutes.
3. Set it aside.
4. Let the pork marinate in the remaining sauce for 2 hours.
5. Afterward, put the pork slices in the basket and set it to AIRBORIL mode 450 degrees for 25 minutes.
6. Make sure the internal temperature is above 160 degrees F once cooked.
7. If not add a few more minutes to the overall cooking time.
8. Once done, take it out and baste it with prepared sauce.
9. Serve and Enjoy.

Serving Suggestion: Serve it with rice

Variation Tip: Skip the wine and add vinegar

Nutritional Information Per Serving: Calories 1239| Fat 73 g| Sodium 2185 mg | Carbs 57.3 g | Fiber 0.4g| Sugar53.7 g | Protein 81.5 g

Ham Burger Patties

Prep: 15 Minutes | Cook Time: 17 Minutes | Makes: 2 Serving

Ingredients

- 1 pound of ground beef
- Salt and pepper, to taste
- ½ teaspoon of red chili powder
- ¼ teaspoon of coriander powder
- 2 tablespoons of chopped onion
- 1 green chili, chopped
- Oil spray for greasing
- 2 large potato wedges

Directions

1. Oil greases the air fryer baskets with oil spray.
2. Add potato wedges in the zone 1 basket.
3. Take a bowl and add minced beef in it and add salt, pepper, chili powder, coriander powder, green chili, and chopped onion.
4. mix well and make two burger patties with wet hands place the two patties in the air fryer zone 2 basket.
5. put the basket inside the air fryer.
6. now, set time for zone 1 for 12 minutes using AIR FRY mode at 400 degrees F.
7. Select the MATCH button for zone 2.
8. once the time of cooking complete, take out the baskets.
9. flip the patties and shake the potatoes wedges.
10. again, set time of zone 1 basket for 4 minutes at 400 degrees F
11. Select the MATCH button for the second basket.
12. Once it's done, serve and enjoy.

Serving Suggestion: Serve it with bread slices, cheese, and pickles, lettuce, and onion

Variation Tip: None

Nutritional Information Per Serving: Calories875 | Fat21.5g | Sodium 622mg | Carbs 88g | Fiber10.9 g| Sugar 3.4g | Protein 78.8g

Pork Chops

Prep: 10 Minutes | Cook Time: 17 Minutes | Makes: 2 Servings

Ingredients

- 1 tablespoon of rosemary, chopped
- Salt and black pepper, to taste
- 2 garlic cloves
- 1-inch ginger
- 2 tablespoons of olive oil
- 8 pork chops

Directions

1. Take a blender and pulse together rosemary, salt, pepper, garlic cloves, ginger, and olive oil.
2. Rub this marinade over pork chops and let it rest for 1 hour.
3. Then divide it amongst air fryer baskets and set it to AIR FRY mode for 17 minutes at 375 degrees F.
4. Once the cooking cycle is done, take out and serve hot.

Serving Suggestion: Serve it with salad

Variation Tip: Use canola oil instead of olive oil

Nutritional Information Per Serving: Calories 1154| Fat 93.8g| Sodium 225mg | Carbs 2.1g | Fiber0.8 g| Sugar 0g | Protein 72.2g

Beef Ribs I

Prep: 10 Minutes | Cook Time: 15 Minutes | Makes: 2 Servings

Ingredients

- 4 tablespoons of barbecue spice rub
- 1 tablespoon kosher salt and black pepper
- 3 tablespoons brown sugar
- 2 pounds of beef ribs (3-3 1/2 pounds), cut in thirds
- 1 cup barbecue sauce

Directions

1. In a small bowl, add salt, pepper, brown sugar, and BBQ spice rub.
2. Grease the ribs with oil spray from both sides and then rub it with a spice mixture.
3. Divide the ribs amongst the basket and set it to AIR FRY MODE at 375 degrees F for 15 minutes.
4. Hit start and let the air fryer cook the ribs.
5. Once done, serve with the coating BBQ sauce.

Serving Suggestion: Serve it with salad and baked potato

Variation Tip: Use sea salt instead of kosher salt

Nutritional Information Per Serving: Calories1081 | Fat 28.6 g| Sodium 1701mg | Carbs 58g | Fiber 0.8g| Sugar 45.7g | Protein 138 g

Beef Ribs II

Prep: 20 Minutes | Cook Time: 1 Hour | Makes: 2 Servings

Ingredients for Marinade

- ¼ cup olive oil
- 4 garlic cloves, minced
- ½ cup white wine vinegar
- ¼ cup soy sauce, reduced-sodium
- ¼ cup Worcestershire sauce
- 1 lemon juice
- Salt and black pepper, to taste
- 2 tablespoons of Italian seasoning
- 1 teaspoon of smoked paprika
- 2 tablespoons of mustard
- ½ cup maple syrup

Meat Ingredients

- Oil spray, for greasing
- 8 beef ribs lean

Directions

1. Take a large bowl and add all the ingredients under marinade ingredients.
2. Put the marinade in a zip lock bag and add ribs to it.
3. Let it sit for 4 hours.
4. Now take out the basket of air fryer and grease the baskets with oil spray.
5. Now dived the ribs among two baskets.
6. Set it to AIR fry mode at 220 degrees F for 30 minutes.
7. Select Pause and take out the baskets.
8. Afterward, flip the ribs and cook for 30 minutes at 250 degrees F.
9. Once done, serve the juicy and tender ribs.
10. Enjoy.

Serving Suggestion: Serve it with Mac and cheese

Variation Tip: Use garlic-infused oil instead of garlic cloves

Nutritional Information Per Serving: Calories 1927| Fat116g| Sodium 1394mg | Carbs 35.2g | Fiber 1.3g| Sugar29 g | Protein 172.3g

Spicy Lamb Chops

Prep: 15 Minutes | Cook Time: 15 Minutes | Makes: 4 Servings

Ingredients

- 12 lamb chops, bone-in
- Salt and black pepper, to taste
- ½ teaspoon of lemon zest
- 1 tablespoon of lemon juice
- 1 teaspoon of paprika
- 1 teaspoon of garlic powder
- ½ teaspoon of Italian seasoning
- ¼ teaspoon of onion powder

Directions

1. Add the lamb chops to the bowl and sprinkle salt, garlic powder, Italian seasoning, onion powder, black pepper, lemon zest, lemon juice, and paprika.
2. Rub the chops well, and divide it between both the baskets of the air fryer.
3. Set zone 1 basket to 400 degrees F, for 15 minutes at AIR FRY mode.
4. Select MATCH for zone2 basket.
5. After 10 minutes, take out the baskets and flip the chops cook for the remaining minutes, and then serve.

Serving Suggestion: Serve it over rice

Variation Tip: None

Nutritional Information Per Serving: Calories 787| Fat 45.3g| Sodium1 mg | Carbs 16.1g | Fiber0.3g | Sugar 0.4g | Protein 75.3g

Yogurt Lamb Chops

Prep: 10 Minutes | Cook Time: 20 Minutes | Makes: 2 Servings

Ingredients

- 1½ cups plain Greek yogurt
- 1 lemon, juice only
- 1 teaspoon ground cumin
- 1 teaspoon ground coriander
- ¾ teaspoon ground turmeric
- ¼ teaspoon ground allspice
- 10 rib lamb chops (1–1¼ inches thick cut)
- 2 tablespoons olive oil, divided

Directions

1. Take a bowl and add lamb chop along with listed ingredients.
2. Rub the lamb chops well.
3. and let it marinate in the refrigerator for 1 hour.
4. Afterward takeout the lamb chops from the refrigerator.
5. Layer parchment paper on top of the baskets of the air fryer.
6. Divide it between ninja air fryer baskets.
7. Set the time for zone 1 to 20 minutes at 400 degrees F.
8. Select the MATCH button for the zone 2 basket.
9. Hit start and then wait for the chop to be cooked.
10. Once the cooking is done, the cool sign will appear on display.
11. Take out the lamb chops and let the chops serve on plates.

Serving Suggestion: Serve over rice

Variation Tip: Use canola oil instead of olive oil

Nutritional Information Per Serving: Calories1973 | Fat90 g| Sodium228 mg | Carbs 109.2g | Fiber 1g | Sugar 77.5g | Protein 184g

Bell Peppers with Sausages

Prep: 15 Minutes | Cook Time: 20 Minutes | Makes: 4 Servings

Ingredients

- 6 beef or pork Italian sausages
- 4 bell peppers, whole
- Oil spray, for greasing
- 2 cups of cooked rice
- 1 cup of sour cream

Directions

1. Put the bell pepper in the zone 1 basket and sausages in the zone 2 basket of the air fryer.
2. Set zone 1 to AIR FRY MODE for 10 minutes at 400 degrees F.
3. For zone 2 set it to 20 minutes at 375 degrees F.
4. Hit the smart finish button, so both finish at the same time.
5. After 5 minutes take out the sausage basket and break or mince it with a plastic spatula.
6. Then, let the cooking cycle finish.
7. Once done serve the minced meat with bell peppers and serve over cooked rice with a dollop of sour cream.

Serving Suggestion: Serve it with salad

Variation Tip: use olive oil instead of oil spray.

Nutritional Information Per Serving: Calories1356 | Fat 81.2g| Sodium 3044 mg | Carbs 96g | Fiber 3.1g | Sugar 8.3g | Protein 57.2 g

Chapter 5-Chicken and Poultry Recipes

Cornish Hen with Baked Potatoes

Prep: 20 Minutes | Cook Time: 45 Minutes | Makes: 2 Servings

Ingredients

- Salt, to taste
- 1 large potato
- 1 tablespoon of avocado oil
- 1.5 pounds of Cornish hen, skinless and whole
- 2-3 teaspoons of poultry seasoning, dry rub

Directions

1. Take a fork and pierce the large potato.
2. Rub the potato with avocado oil and salt.
3. Now put the potatoes in the first basket.
4. Now pick the Cornish hen and season the hen with poultry seasoning (dry rub) and salt.
5. Remember to coat the whole Cornish hen well.
6. Put the potato in zone 1 basket.
7. Now place the hen into zone 2 baskets.
8. Now hit 1 for the first basket and set it to AIR FRY mode at 350 degrees F, for 45 minutes.
9. For the second basket hit 2 and set the time to 45 minutes at 350 degrees F.
10. To start cooking, hit the smart finish button and press hit start.
11. Once the cooking cycle complete, turn off the air fryer and take out the potatoes and Cornish hen from both air fryer baskets.
12. Serve hot and enjoy.

Serving Suggestion: Serve it with Coleslaw

Variation Tip: You can use olive oil or canola oil instead of avocado oil.

Nutritional Information Per Serving: Calories 612 | Fat14.3 g| Sodium 304mg | Carbs33.4 g | Fiber 4.5 g | Sugar 1.5g | Protein 83.2 g

Cornish Hen with Asparagus

Prep: 20 Minutes | Cook Time: 45 Minutes | Makes: 2 Servings

Ingredients

- 10 spears of asparagus
- Salt and black pepper, to taste
- 1 Cornish hen
- Salt, to taste
- Black pepper, to taste
- 1 teaspoon of Paprika
- Coconut spray, for greasing
- 2 lemons, sliced

Directions

1. Wash and pat dry the asparagus and coat it with coconut oil spray.
2. Sprinkle salt on the asparagus and place inside the first basket of the air fryer.
3. Next, take the Cornish hen and rub it well with the salt, black pepper, and paprika.
4. Oil sprays the Cornish hen and place in the second air fryer basket.
5. Press button 1 for the first basket and set it to AIR FRY mode at 350 degrees F, for 8 minutes.
6. For the second basket hit 2 and set the time to 45 minutes at 350 degrees F, by selecting the ROAST mode.
7. To start cooking, hit the smart finish button and press hit start.
8. Once the 6 minutes pass press 1 and pause and take out the asparagus.
9. Once the chicken cooking cycle complete, press 2 and hit pause.
10. Take out the Basket of chicken and let it transfer to the serving plate
11. Serve the chicken with roasted asparagus and slices of lemon.
12. Serve hot and enjoy.

Serving Suggestion: Serve it with ranch dressing

Variation Tip: You can add variation by choosing chopped cilantro instead of a lemon slice.

Nutritional Information Per Serving: Calories 192| Fat 4.7g| Sodium 151mg | Carbs10.7 g | Fiber 4.6g | Sugar 3.8g | Protein 30g

Chicken Thighs with Brussels sprouts

Prep: 20 Minutes | Cook Time: 30 Minutes | Makes: 2 Servings

Ingredients

- 2 tablespoons of honey
- 4 tablespoons of Dijon mustard
- Salt and black pepper, to tat
- 4 tablespoons of olive oil
- 1-1/2 cup Brussels sprouts
- 8 chicken thighs, skinless

Directions

1. Take a bowl and add chicken thighs to it.
2. Add honey, Dijon mustard, salt, pepper, and 2 tablespoons of olive oil to the thighs.
3. Coat the chicken well and marinate it for 1 hour.
4. Now when start cooking season the Brussels sprouts with salt and black pepper along with remaining olive oil.
5. Put the chicken in the zone 1 basket.
6. Put the Brussels sprouts into the zone 2 basket.
7. Select ROAST function for chicken and set time to 30 minutes at 390 degrees F.
8. Select AIR FRY function for Brussels sprouts and set the timer to 20 at 400 degrees F.
9. Once done, serve and enjoy.

Serving Suggestion: Serve it with Barbecue Sauce

Variation Tip: You can use canola oil instead of olive oil.

Nutritional Information Per Serving: Calories1454 | Fat 72.2g| Sodium 869mg | Carbs 23g | Fiber 2.7g | Sugar 19g | Protein 172g

Chicken & Broccoli

Prep: 22 Minutes | Cook Time: 35 Minutes | Makes: 2 Servings

Ingredients

- 1 pound of chicken, boneless & bite-size pieces
- 1-1/2 cup of broccoli
- 2 tablespoons of Grape seed oil
- 1/3 teaspoon of garlic powder
- 1 teaspoon of ginger and garlic paste
- 2 teaspoons of soy sauce
- 1 tablespoon of sesame seed oil
- 2 teaspoons rice vinegar
- Salt and black pepper, to taste
- Oil spray, for coating

Directions

1. Take a small bowl and whisk together Grape seed oil, ginger and garlic paste, sesame seeds oil, rice vinegar, and soy sauce.
2. Take a large bowl and mix chicken pieces with the prepared marinade.
3. Let it sit for 1 hour.
4. Now, slightly grease the broccoli with oil spray and season it with salt and black pepper.
5. Put the broccoli into the first basket and grease it with oil spray.
6. Put the chicken into the second basket.
7. Press button 1 for the first basket and set it to AIR FRY mode at 350 for 8 minutes.
8. For the second basket hit 2 and set the time to 35 minutes.
9. To start cooking hit the smart finish button and press hit start.
10. Now press 1 and press the pauses and takes out the broccoli.
11. Keep continuing with the chicken cooking process.
12. Once the cooking time completes, take out the chicken and serve it with the broccoli.

Serving Suggestion: Serve it with lemon wedges

Variation Tip: A light oil alternative can be used as grape seed oil.

Nutritional Information Per Serving: Calories588 | Fat 32.1g| Sodium 457mg | Carbs 4g | Fiber1.3 g | Sugar 1g | Protein67.4 g

Wings with Corn on Cob

Prep: 15 Minutes | Cook Time: 40 Minutes | Makes: 2 Servings

Ingredients

- 6 chicken wings, skinless
- 2 tablespoons of coconut amino
- 2 tablespoons of brown sugar
- 1 teaspoon of ginger, paste
- ½ inch garlic, minced
- Salt and black pepper to taste
- 2 corn on cobs, small
- Oil spray, for greasing

Directions

1. Spay the corns with oil spray and season them with salt.
2. Rub the ingredients well.
3. Coat the chicken wings with coconut amino, brown sugar, ginger, garlic, salt, and black pepper.
4. Spray the wings with a good amount of oil spray.
5. Now put the chicken wings in the zone 1 basket.
6. Put the corn into the zone 2 basket.
7. Select ROAST function for chicken wings, press 1, and set time to 23 minutes at 400 degrees F.

8. Press 2 and select the AIR FRY function for corn and set the timer to 40 at 300 degrees F.
9. Once it's done, serve and enjoy.

Serving Suggestion: Serve it with garlic butter sauce

Variation Tip: use butter instead of oil spray.

Nutritional Information Per Serving: Calories 950| Fat33.4g | Sodium592 mg | Carbs27. 4g | Fiber2.1g | Sugar11.3 g | Protein129 g

Spiced Chicken and Vegetables

Prep: 22 Minutes | Cook Time: 45 Minutes | Makes: 1 Serving

Ingredients

- 2 large chicken breasts
- 2 teaspoons of olive oil
- 1 teaspoon of chili powder
- 1 teaspoon of paprika powder
- 1 teaspoon of onion powder
- ½ teaspoon of garlic powder
- 1/4 teaspoon of Cumin
- Salt and black pepper, to taste

Vegetable Ingredients

- 2 large potato, cubed
- 4 large carrots cut into bite-size pieces
- 1 tablespoon of olive oil
- Salt and black pepper, to taste

Directions

1. Take chicken breast pieces and rub olive oil, salt, pepper, chili powder, onion powder, cumin, garlic powder, and paprika.
2. Season the vegetables with olive oil, salt, and black pepper.
3. Now put the chicken breast pieces in the zone 1 basket.
4. Put the vegetables into the zone 2 basket.
5. Now hit 1 for the first basket and set it to ROAST at 350 degrees F, for 45 minutes.
6. For the second basket hit 2 and set time for 45 minutes, by selecting AIR FRY mode at 350 degrees F.
7. To start cooking hit the smart finish button and press hit start.
8. Once the cooking cycle is done, serve, and enjoy.

Serving Suggestion: Serve it with salad or ranch dressing

Variation Tip: Use Canola oil instead of olive oil.

Nutritional Information Per Serving: Calories1510 | Fat 51.3g| Sodium 525mg | Carbs 163g | Fiber24.7 g | Sugar 21.4g | Protein 102.9

Glazed Thighs with French Fries

Prep: 22 Minutes | Cook Time: 35 Minutes | Makes: 3 Servings

Ingredients

- 2 tablespoons of Soy Sauce
- Salt, to taste
- 1 teaspoon of Worcestershire Sauce
- 2 teaspoons Brown Sugar
- 1 teaspoon of Ginger, paste
- 1 teaspoon of Garlic, paste
- 6 Boneless Chicken Thighs
- 1 pound of hand-cut potato fries
- 2 tablespoons of canola oil

Directions

1. Coat the French fries well with canola oil.
2. Season it with salt.
3. In a small bowl, combine the soy sauce, Worcestershire sauce, brown sugar, ginger, and garlic.
4. Place the chicken in this marinade and let it sit for 40 minutes.
5. Put the chicken thighs into the zone 1 basket and fries into the zone 2 basket.
6. Press button 1 for the first basket, and set it to ROAST mode at 350 degrees F for 35 minutes.
7. For the second basket hit 2 and set time to 30 minutes at 360 degrees F, by selecting AIR FRY mode.
8. Once the cooking cycle completely take out the fries and chicken and serve it hot.

Serving Suggestion: Serve it with ketchup

Variation Tip: You can use honey instead of brown sugar

Nutritional Information Per Serving: Calories 858| Fat39g | Sodium 1509mg | Carbs 45.6g | Fiber 4.4g | Sugar3 g | Protein 90g

Sweet and Spicy Carrots with Chicken Thighs

Prep: 15 Minutes | Cook Time: 35 Minutes | Makes: 2 Servings

Ingredients

Ingredients for Glaze

- Cooking spray, for greasing
- 2 tablespoons butter, melted
- 1 tablespoon hot honey
- 1 teaspoon orange zest
- 1 teaspoon cardamom
- ½ pound baby carrots
- 1 tablespoon orange juice
- Salt and black pepper, to taste

Other Ingredients

- ½ pound of carrots, baby carrots
- 8 chicken thighs

Directions

1. Take a bowl and mix all the glaze ingredients in it.
2. Now, coat the chicken and carrots with the glaze and let it rest for 30 minutes.
3. Now place the chicken thighs into the zone 1 basket.
4. Next put the glazed carrots into the zone 2 basket.
5. Press button 1 for the first basket and set it to ROAST Mode at 350 degrees F for 35 minutes.
6. For the second basket hit 2 and set time to AIRFRY mode at 390 degrees F for 8-10 minutes.
7. Once the cooking cycle completes take out the carrots and chicken and serve it hot.

Serving Suggestion: Serve with Salad

Variation Tip: Use lime juice instead of orange juice.

Nutritional Information Per Serving: Calories 1312| Fat 55.4g| Sodium 757mg | Carbs 23.3g | Fiber6.7 g | Sugar12 g | Protein171 g

Spice-Rubbed Chicken Pieces

Prep: 22 Minutes | Cook Time: 40 Minutes | Makes: 6 Servings

Ingredients

- 3 pounds chicken, pieces
- 1 teaspoon sweet paprika
- 1 teaspoon mustard powder
- 1 tablespoon brown sugar, dark
- Salt and black pepper, to taste
- 1 teaspoon Chile powder, New Mexico
- 1 teaspoon oregano, dried
- ¼ teaspoon allspice powder, ground

Directions

1. Take a bowl and mix dark brown sugar, salt, paprika, mustard powder, oregano, Chile powder, black pepper, and all spice powder.
2. Mix well and rub this spice mixture all over the chicken.
3. Divide the chicken between two air fryer baskets.
4. Oil sprays the meat and then adds it to the air fryer.
5. Now press button1 and button 2 and set the time to 40 minutes at 350 degrees F.
6. Now press start and once the cooking cycle completes, press pause for both the zones.
7. Take out the chicken and serve hot.

Serving Suggestion: Serve it with coleslaw, peanut sauce, or ranch

Variation Tip: use light brown sugar instead of dark brown sugar.

Nutritional Information Per Serving: Calories353 | Fat 7.1g| Sodium400 mg | Carbs 2.2g | Fiber0.4 g | Sugar 1.6g | Protein66 g

Spicy Chicken

Prep: 12 Minutes | Cook Time: 35-40 Minutes | Makes: 4 Servings

Ingredients

- 4 chicken thighs
- 2 cups of butter milk
- 4 chicken legs
- 2 cups of flour
- Salt and black pepper, to taste
- 2 tablespoons garlic powder
- ½ teaspoon onion powder
- 1 teaspoon poultry seasoning
- 1 teaspoon cumin
- 2 tablespoons paprika
- 1 tablespoon olive oil

Directions

1. Take a bowl and add buttermilk to it.
2. Soak the chicken thighs and chicken legs in the buttermilk for 2 hours.
3. Mix flour, all the seasonings, and olive oil in a small bowl.
4. Take out the chicken pieces from the buttermilk mixture and then dredge them into the flour mixture.
5. Repeat the steps for all the pieces and then arrange them into both the air fryer basket.
6. Set the timer for both the basket by selecting a roast mode for 35-40 minutes at 350 degrees F.
7. Once the cooking cycle complete select the pause button and then take out the basket.
8. Serve and enjoy.

Serving Suggestion: Serve the chicken with garlic dipping sauce

Variation Tip: Use canola oil instead of olive oil

Nutritional Information Per Serving: Calories 624| Fat17.6 g| Sodium300 mg | Carbs 60g | Fiber 3.5g | Sugar 7.7g | Protein54.2 g

Chicken Breast Strips

Prep: 10 Minutes | Cook Time: 22 Minutes | Makes: 2 Servings

Ingredient

- 2 large organic egg
- 1-ounce buttermilk
- 1 cup of cornmeal
- ¼ cup all-purpose flour
- Salt and black pepper, to taste
- 1 pound of chicken breasts, cut into strips
- 2 tablespoons of oil bay seasoning
- oil spray, for greasing

Directions

1. Take a medium bowl and whisk eggs with buttermilk.
2. In a separate large bowl mix flour, cornmeal, salt, black pepper, and oil bay seasoning.
3. First, dip the chicken breast strip in egg wash and then dredge into the flour mixture.
4. Coat the strip all over and layer on both the baskets that are already grease with oil spray.
5. Grease the chicken breast strips with oil spray as well.
6. Set the zone 1 basket to AIR FRY mode at 400 degrees F for 22 minutes.
7. Select the MATCH button for zone 2.
8. Hit the start button to let the cooking start.
9. Once the cooking cycle is done, serve.

Serving Suggestion: Serve it with roasted vegetables

Variation Tip: None

Nutritional Information Per Serving: Calories 788| Fat25g| Sodium835 mg | Carbs60g | Fiber 4.9g| Sugar1.5g | Protein79g

Yummy Chicken Breasts

Prep: 15 Minutes | Cook Time: 25 Minutes | Makes: 2 Servings

Ingredients

- 4 large chicken breasts, 6 ounces each
- 2 tablespoons of oil bay seasoning
- 1 tablespoon Montreal chicken seasoning
- 1 teaspoon of thyme
- 1/2 teaspoon of paprika
- Salt, to taste
- oil spray, for greasing

Directions

1. Season the chicken breast pieces with the listed seasoning and let them rest for 40 minutes.
2. Grease both sides of the chicken breast pieces with oil spray.
3. Divide the chicken breast piece between both baskets.
4. Set zone 1 to AIRFRY mode at 400 degrees F, for 15 minutes.
5. Select the MATCH button for another basket.
6. Select pause and take out the baskets and flip the chicken breast pieces, after 15 minutes.
7. Select the zones to 400 degrees F for 10 more minutes using the MATCH cook button.
8. Once it's done serve.

Serving Suggestion: Serve it with baked potato

Variation Tip: None

Nutritional Information Per Serving: Calories 711| Fat 27.7g| Sodium 895mg | Carbs 1.6g | Fiber 0.4g | Sugar 0.1g | Protein 106.3g

Chicken Wings

Prep: 15 Minutes | Cook Time: 20 Minutes | Makes: 3 Servings

Ingredients

- 1 cup chicken batter mix, Louisiana
- 9 Chicken wings
- ½ teaspoon of smoked paprika
- 2 tablespoons of Dijon mustard
- 1 tablespoon of cayenne pepper
- 1 teaspoon of meat tenderizer, powder
- oil spray, for greasing

Directions

1. Pat dry chicken wings and add mustard, paprika, meat tenderizer, and cayenne pepper.
2. Dredge it in the chicken batter mix.
3. Oil sprays the chicken wings.
4. Grease both baskets of the air fryer.
5. Divide the wings between the two zones of the air fryer.
6. Set zone 1 to AR FRY mode at 400 degrees F for 20 minutes
7. Select MATCH for zone 2.
8. Hit start to begin with the cooking.
9. Once the cooking cycle complete, serve, and enjoy hot.

Serving Suggestion: Serve it with salad

Variation Tip: use American yellow mustard instead of Dijon mustard

Nutritional Information Per Serving: Calories621 | Fat 32.6g| Sodium 2016mg | Carbs 46.6g | Fiber 1.1g | Sugar 0.2g | Protein 32.1g

Chicken Leg Piece

Prep: 15 Minutes | Cook Time: 25 Minutes | Makes: 1 Serving

Ingredients

- 1 teaspoon of onion powder
- 1 teaspoon of paprika powder
- 1 teaspoon of garlic powder
- Salt and black pepper, to taste
- 1 tablespoon of Italian seasoning
- 1 teaspoon of celery seeds
- 2 eggs, whisked
- 1/3 cup buttermilk
- 1 cup of corn flour
- 1 pound of chicken leg

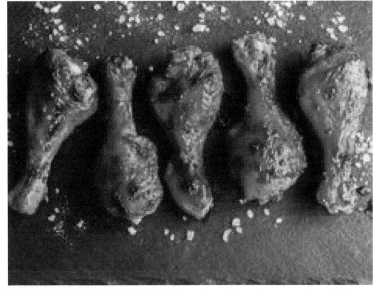

Directions

1. Take a bowl and whisk egg along with pepper, salt, and buttermilk.
2. Set it aside for further use.
3. Mix all the spices in a small separate bowl.
4. Dredge the chicken in egg wash then dredge it in seasoning.
5. Coat the chicken legs with oil spray.
6. At the end dust it with the corn flour.
7. Divide the leg pieces into two zones.
8. Set zone 1 basket to 400 degrees F, for 25 minutes.
9. Select MATCH for zone 2 basket.
10. Let the air fryer do the magic.
11. Once it's done, serve and enjoy.

Serving Suggestion: Serve it with cooked rice

Variation Tip: Use water instead of buttermilk.

Nutritional Information Per Serving: Calories 1511| Fat 52.3g| Sodium615 mg | Carbs 100g | Fiber 9.2g | Sugar 8.1g | Protein 154.2g

Chapter 6-Seafood and Fish Recipes

Fish and Chips

Prep: 15 Minutes | Cook Time: 22 Minutes | Makes: 2 Servings

Ingredients

- 1 pound of potatoes, cut lengthwise
- 1 cup seasoned flour
- 2 eggs, organic
- 1/3 cup buttermilk
- 2 cup seafood fry mix
- ½ cup bread crumbs
- 2 codfish fillet, 6 ounces each
- Oil spray, for greasing

Directions

1. take a bowl and whisk eggs in it along   buttermilk.
2. In a separate bowl mix seafood fry mix and bread crumbs
3. Take a baking tray and spread flour on it
4. Dip the fillets first in egg wash, then in flour, and at the end coat it with breadcrumbs mixture.
5. Put the fish fillet in air fryer zone 1 basket.
6. Grease the fish fillet with oil spray.
7. Set zone 1 to AIR FRY mode at 400 degrees F for 14 minutes.
8. Put potato chip in zone two baskets and lightly grease it with oil spray.
9. Set the zone 2 basket to AIRFRY mode at 400 degrees F for 22 minutes.
10. Hit the smart finish button.
11. Once done, serve and enjoy.

Serving Suggestion: Serve it with mayonnaise

Variation Tip: use water instead of buttermilk

Nutritional Information Per Serving: Calories 992| Fat 22.3g| Sodium1406 mg | Carbs 153.6g | Fiber 10g | Sugar10 g | Protein 40g

Beer Battered Fish Fillet

Prep: 18 Minutes | Cook Time: 14 Minutes | Makes: 2 Servings

Ingredients

- 1 cup all-purpose flour
- 4 tablespoons cornstarch
- 1 teaspoon baking soda
- 8 ounces beer
- 2 egg beaten
- ½ cup all-purpose flour
- 1 teaspoon smoked paprika
- 1 teaspoon salt
- 1/4 teaspoon freshly ground black pepper
- ¼ teaspoon of cayenne pepper
- 2 cod fillets, 1½-inches thick, cut into 4 pieces
- Oil spray, for greasing

Directions

1. Take a large bowl and combine flour, baking soda, corn starch, and salt
2. In a separate bowl beat eggs along with the beer.
3. In a shallow dish mix paprika, salt, pepper, and cayenne pepper.
4. Dry the codfish fillets with a paper towel.
5. Dip the fish into the eggs and coat it with seasoned flour.
6. Then dip it in the seasoning.
7. Grease the fillet with oil spray.
8. Divide the fillet between both zones.
9. Set zone 1 to AIR FRY mode at 400 degrees F for 14 minutes.
10. Select MACTH button for zone 2 basket.
11. Press start and let the AIR fry do its magic.
12. Once cooking is done, serve the fish.
13. Enjoy it hot.

Serving Suggestion: Serve it with rice

Variation Tip: Use mild paprika instead of smoked paprika

Nutritional Information Per Serving: Calories 1691| Fat 6.1g| Sodium 3976mg | Carbs105.1 g | Fiber 3.4g | Sugar15.6 g | Protein 270g

Frozen Breaded Fish Fillet

Prep: 15 Minutes | Cook Time: 12 Minutes | Makes: 2 Servings

Ingredients

- 4 Frozen Breaded Fish Fillet
- Oil spray, for greasing
- 1 cup mayonnaise

Directions

1. Take the frozen fish fillets out of the bag and place them in both baskets of the air fryer.
2. Lightly grease it with oil spray.
3. Set the Zone 1 basket to 380 degrees F fo12 minutes.
4. Select the MATCH button for the zone 2 basket.
5. hit the start button to start cooking.
6. Once the cooking is done, serve the fish hot with mayonnaise.

Serving Suggestion: Serve it with salad and rice

Variation Tip: Use olive oil instead of butter

Nutritional Information Per Serving: Calories 921| Fat 61.5g| Sodium 1575mg | Carbs 69g | Fiber 2g | Sugar 9.5g | Protein 29.1g

Two-Way Salmon

Prep: 10 Minutes | Cook Time: 18 Minutes | Makes: 2 Servings

Ingredients

- 2 salmon fillets, 8 ounces each
- 2 tablespoons of Cajun seasoning
- 2 tablespoons of jerk seasoning
- 1 lemon cut in half
- oil spray, for greasing

Directions

1. First, drizzle lemon juice over the salmon and wash it with tap water.
2. Rinse and pat dry the fillets with a paper towel.
3. Now rub o fillet with Cajun seasoning and grease it with oil spray.
4. Take the second fillet and rub it with jerk seasoning.
5. Grease the second fillet of salmon with oil spray.
6. now put the salmon fillets in both the baskets.
7. Set the Zone 1 basket to 390 degrees F for 16-18 minutes
8. Select MATCH button for zone 2 basket.
9. hit the start button to start cooking.
10. Once the cooking is done, serve the fish hot with mayonnaise.

Serving Suggestion: Serve it with ranch

Variation Tip: None

Nutritional Information Per Serving: Calories 238| Fat 11.8g| Sodium 488mg | Carbs 9g | Fiber 0g | Sugar8 g | Protein 35g

Salmon with Green Beans

Prep: 12 Minutes | Cook Time: 18 Minutes | Makes: 1 Serving

Ingredients

- 1 salmon fillet, 2 inches thick
- 2 teaspoons of olive oil
- 2 teaspoons of smoked paprika
- Salt and black pepper, to taste
- 1 cup green beans
- Oil spray, for greasing

Directions

1. Grease the green beans with oil spray and add them to zone 1 basket.
2. Now rub the salmon fillet with olive oil, smoked paprika, salt, and black pepper.
3. Put the salmon fillets in the zone 2 basket.
4. Now set the zone one basket to AIRFRY mode at 350 degrees F for 18 minutes.
5. Set the Zone 2 basket to 390 degrees F for 16-18 minutes
6. Hit the smart finish button.
7. Once done, take out the salmon and green beans and transfer them to the serving plates and enjoy.

Serving Suggestion: Serve it with ranch

Variation Tip: Use any other green vegetable of your choice

Nutritional Information Per Serving: Calories 367| Fat22 g| Sodium 87mg | Carbs 10.2g | Fiber 5.3g | Sugar 2g | Protein 37.2g

Spicy Fish Fillet with Onion Rings

Prep: 10 Minutes | Cook Time: 12 Minutes | Makes:1 Serving

Ingredients

- 300 grams of onion rings, frozen and packed
- 1 codfish fillet, 8 ounces
- Salt and black pepper, to taste
- 1 teaspoon of lemon juice
- oil spray, for greasing

Directions

1. Put the frozen onion rings in zone 1 basket of the air fryer.
2. Next pat dry the fish fillets with a paper towel and season them with salt, black pepper, and lemon juice.
3. Grease the fillet with oil spray.
4. Put the fish in zone 2 basket.
5. Use MAX crisp for zone 1 at 240 degrees for 9 minutes.
6. Use MAX crisp for zone 2 basket and set it to 210 degrees for 12 minutes.
7. Press sync and press start.
8. Once done, serve hot.

Serving Suggestion: Serve with buffalo sauce

Variation Tip: None

Nutritional Information Per Serving: Calories 666| Fat23.5g| Sodium 911mg | Carbs 82g | Fiber 8.8g | Sugar 17.4g | Protein 30.4g

Keto Baked Salmon with Pesto

Prep: 15 Minutes | Cook Time: 18 Minutes | Makes: 2 Servings

Ingredients

- 4 salmon fillets, 2 inches thick
- 2 ounces green pesto
- Salt and black pepper
- ½ tablespoon of canola oil, for greasing

Ingredients for Green Sauce

- 1-1/2 cup mayonnaise
- 2 tablespoons Greek yogurt
- Salt and black pepper, to taste

Directions

1. Rub the salmon with pesto, salt, oil, and black pepper.
2. In a small bowl, whisk together all the green sauce ingredients.
3. Divide the fish fillets between both the baskets.
4. Set zone 1 to air fry mode for 18 minutes at 390 degrees F.
5. Select MATCH button for Zone 2 basket.
6. Once the cooking is done, serve it with green sauce drizzle.
7. Enjoy.

Serving Suggestion: Serve it with mashed cheesy potatoes

Variation Tip: Use butter instead of canal oil

Nutritional Information Per Serving: Calories 1165 | Fat80.7 g| Sodium 1087 mg | Carbs 33.1g | Fiber 0.5g | Sugar11.5 g | Protein 80.6g

Salmon with Broccoli and Cheese

Prep: 15 Minutes | Cook Time: 18 Minutes | Makes: 2 Servings

Ingredients

- 2 cups of broccoli
- ½ cup of butter, melted
- Salt and pepper, to taste
- Oil spray, for greasing
- 1 cup of grated cheddar cheese
- 1 pound of salmon, fillets

Directions

1. Take a bowl and add broccoli to it.
2. Add salt and black pepper and spray it with oil.
3. Put the broccoli in the air fryer zone 1 backset.
4. Now rub the salmon fillets with salt, black pepper, and butter.
5. Put it into zone 2 baskets.
6. Set zone 1 to air fry mode for 5 minters at 400 degrees F.
7. Set zone 2 to air fry mode for 18 minutes at 390 degrees F.
8. Hit start to start the cooking.
9. Once done, serve and by placing it on serving plates.
10. Put the grated cheese on top of the salmon and serve.

Serving Suggestion: Serve it with rice and baked potato

Variation Tip: Use olive oil instead of butter

Nutritional Information Per Serving: Calories 966 | Fat 79.1 g| Sodium 808 mg | Carbs 6.8 g | Fiber 2.4g | Sugar 1.9g | Protein 61.2 g

Lemon Pepper Salmon with Asparagus

Prep: 20 Minutes | Cook Time: 18 Minutes | Makes: 2 Servings

Ingredients

- 1 cup of green asparagus
- 2 tablespoons of butter
- 2 fillets of salmon, 8 ounces each
- Salt and black pepper, to taste
- 1 teaspoon of lemon juice
- ½ teaspoon of lemon zest
- oil spray, for greasing

Directions

1. Rinse and trim the asparagus.
2. Rinse and pat dry the salmon fillets.
3. Take a bowl and mix lemon juice, lemon zest, salt, and black pepper.
4. Brush the fish fillet with the rub and place it in the zone 1 basket.
5. Place asparagus in zone 2 basket.
6. Spray the asparagus with oil spray.
7. Set zone 1 to AIRFRY mode for 18 minutes at 390 degrees F.
8. Set the zone 2 to 5 minutes at 390 degrees F, at air fry mode.
9. Hit the smart finish button to finish at the same time.
10. Once done, serve and enjoy.

Serving Suggestion: Serve it with baked potato

Variation Tip: Use olive oil instead of butter.

Nutritional Information Per Serving: Calories 482| Fat 28g| Sodium209 mg | Carbs 2.8g | Fiber1.5 g | Sugar1.4 g | Protein 56.3g

Salmon with Coconut

Prep: 10 Minutes | Cook Time: 15 Minutes | Makes: 2 Servings

Ingredients

- Oil spray, for greasing
- 2 salmon fillets, 6ounces each
- Salt and ground black pepper, to taste
- 1 tablespoon butter, for frying
- 1 tablespoon red curry paste
- 1 cup of coconut cream
- 2 tablespoons fresh cilantro, chopped
- 1 cup of cauliflower florets
- ½ cup Parmesan cheese, hard

Directions

1. Take a bowl and mix salt, black pepper, butter, red curry paste, coconut cream in a bowl and marinate the salmon in it.
2. Oil sprays the cauliflower florets and then seasons it with salt and freshly ground black pepper.
3. Put the florets in the zone 1 basket.
4. Layer the parchment paper over the zone 2 baskets, and then place the salmon fillet on it.
5. Set the zone 2 basket to AIR FRY mod at 15 minutes for4 00 degrees F
6. Hit the smart finish button to finish it at the same time.
7. Once the time for cooking is over, serve the salmon with cauliflower floret with Parmesan cheese drizzle on top.

Serving Suggestion: Serve it with rice

Variation Tip: use mozzarella cheese instead of Parmesan cheese

Nutritional Information Per Serving: Calories 774 | Fat 59g| Sodium 1223mg | Carbs 12.2g | Fiber 3.9g | Sugar5.9 g | Protein53.5 g

Seafood Shrimp Omelet

Prep: 20 Minutes | Cook Time: 15 Minutes | Makes: 2 Servings

Ingredient

- 6 large shrimp, shells removed and chopped
- 6 eggs, beaten
- ½ tablespoon of butter, melted
- 2 tablespoons green onions, sliced
- 1/3 cup of mushrooms, chopped
- 1 pinch paprika
- Salt and black pepper, to taste
- Oil spray, for greasing

Directions

1. In a large bowl whisk the eggs and add chopped shrimp, butter, green onions, mushrooms, paprika, salt, and black pepper.
2. Take two cake pans that fit inside the air fryer and grease them with oil spray.
3. Pour the egg mixture between the cake pans and place it in two baskets of the air fryer.
4. Turn on the BAKE function of zone 1, and let it cook for 15 minutes at 320 degrees F.
5. Select the MATCH button to match the cooking time for the zone 2 basket.
6. Once the cooking cycle completes, take out, and serve hot.

Serving Suggestion: Serve it with rice

Variation Tip: use olive oil for greasing purposes

Nutritional Information Per Serving: Calories 300 | Fat 17.5g| Sodium 368mg | Carbs 2.9g | Fiber 0.3g | Sugar1.4 g | Protein32.2 g

Smoked Salmon

Prep: 20 Minutes | Cook Time: 12 Minutes | Makes: 4 Servings

Ingredients

- 2 pounds of salmon fillets, smoked
- 6 ounces cream cheese
- 4 tablespoons mayonnaise
- 2 teaspoons of chives, fresh
- 1 teaspoon of lemon zest
- Salt and freshly ground black pepper, to taste
- 2 tablespoons of butter

Directions

1. Cut the salmon into very small and uniform bite-size pieces.
2. Mix cream cheese, chives, mayonnaise, black pepper, and lemon zest, in a small mixing bowl.
3. Let it sit aside for further use.
4. Coat the salmon pieces with salt and butter.
5. Divide the bite-size pieces into both zones of the air fryer.
6. Set it on AIRFRY mode at 400 degrees F for 12 minutes.
7. Select MATCH for zone 2 basket.
8. Hit start, so the cooking start.
9. Once the salmon is done, top it with a bowl creamy mixture and serve.
10. Enjoy hot.

Serving Suggestion: Serve it with rice

Variation Tip: use sour cream instead of cream cheese

Nutritional Information Per Serving: Calories 557| Fat 15.7 g| Sodium 371mg | Carbs 4.8 g | Fiber 0g | Sugar 1.1g | Protein 48 g

Codfish with Herb Vinaigrette

Prep: 15 Minutes | Cook Time: 16 Minutes | Makes: 2 Servings

Ingredients

Vinaigrette Ingredients

- 1/2 cup parsley leaves
- 1 cup basil leaves
- ½ cup mint leaves
- 2 tablespoons   thyme leaves
- 1/4 teaspoon red pepper flakes
- 2 cloves of garlic
- 4 tablespoons of red wine vinegar
- ¼ cup of olive oil
- Salt, to taste

Other Ingredients

- 1.5 pounds fish fillets, cod fish
- 2 tablespoons olive oil
- Salt and black pepper, to taste
- 1 teaspoon of paprika
- 1teasbpoon of Italian seasoning

Directions

1. Blend the entire vinaigrette ingredient in a high-speed blender and pulse into a smooth paste.
2. Set aside for drizzling overcooked fish.
3. Rub the fillets with salt, black pepper, paprika, Italian seasoning, and olive oil.
4. Divide it between two baskets of the air fryer.
5. Set the zone 1 to 16 minutes at 390 degrees F, at AIR FRY mode.
6. Press the MATCH button for the second basket.
7. Once done, serve the fillets with the drizzle of blended vinaigrette

Serving Suggestion: Serve it with rice

Variation Tip: use sour cream instead of cream cheese

Nutritional Information Per Serving: Calories 1219| Fat 81.8g| Sodium 1906mg | Carbs64.4 g | Fiber5.5 g | Sugar 0.4g | Protein 52.1g

Chapter 7-Vegetables Recipes

Fresh Mix Veggies in Air Fryer

Prep: 15minutes | Cook Time: 12 Minutes | Makes: 4 Servings

Ingredients

- 1 cup cauliflower florets
- 1 cup of carrots, peeled chopped
- 1 cup broccoli florets
- 2 tablespoons of avocado oil
- Salt, to taste
- ½ teaspoon of chili powder
- ½ teaspoon of garlic powder
- ½ teaspoon of herbs de Provence
- 1 cup parmesan cheese

Directions

1. Take a bowl, and add all the veggies to it.
2. Toss and then season the veggies with salt, chili powder, garlic powder, and herbs de Provence.
3. Toss it all well and then drizzle avocado oil.
4. Make sure the ingredients are coated well.
5. Now distribute the veggies among both baskets of the air fryer.
6. Turn on the start button and set it to AIR FRY mode at 390 degrees for 10-12 minutes.
7. For the zone 2 basket setting, press the MATCH button.
8. After 8 minutes of cooking, select the pause button and then take out the baskets and sprinkle Parmesan cheese on top of the veggies.
9. Then let the cooking cycle complete for the next 3-4 minutes.
10. Once done, serve.

Serving Suggestion: Serve it with rice

Variation Tip: Use canola oil or Butter instead of avocado oil

Nutritional Information Per Serving: Calories161 | Fat 9.3g| Sodium434 mg | Carbs 7.7g | Fiber 2.4g | Sugar 2.5g | Protein 13.9

Garlic Potato Wedges in Air Fryer

Prep: 10 Minutes | Cook Time: 23 Minutes | Makes: 2 Servings

Ingredients

- 4 medium potatoes, peeled and cut into wedges
- 4 tablespoons of butter
- 1 teaspoon of chopped cilantro
- 1 cup plain flour
- 1 teaspoon of garlic, minced
- Salt and black pepper, to taste

Directions

1. Soak the potatoes wedges in cold water for about 30 minutes.
2. Then drain and pat dry with a paper towel.
3. Boil water in a large pot and boil the wedges just for 3 minutes.
4. Then take it out on a paper towel.
5. Now in a bowl mix garlic, melted butter, salt, pepper, cilantro and whisk it well.
6. Add the flour to a separate bowl and add salt and black pepper.
7. Then add water to the flour so it gets runny in texture.
8. Now, coat the potatoes with flour mixture and add it to two foil tins.
9. Put foil tins in both the air fryer basket.
10. Now, set time for zone 1 basket using AIRFRY mode at 390 degrees F for 20 minutes.
11. Select the MATCH button for the zone 2 basket.
12. Once done, serve and enjoy.

Serving Suggestion: Serve with ketchup

Variation Tip: use olive oil instead of butter

Nutritional Information Per Serving: Calories 727| Fat 24.1g| Sodium 191mg | Carbs 115.1g | Fiber 12g | Sugar 5.1g | Protein14 g

Mixed Air Fry Veggies

Prep: 15 Minutes | Cook Time: 25 Minutes | Makes: 4 Servings

Ingredients

- 2 cups of carrots, cubed
- 2 cups of potatoes, cubed
- 2 cups of shallots, cubed
- 2 cups zucchini, diced
- 2 cups yellow squash, cubed
- Salt and black pepper, to taste
- 1 tablespoon of Italian seasoning
- 2 tablespoons of ranch seasoning
- 4 tablespoons of olive oil

Directions

1. Take a large bowl and add all the veggies to it.
2. Season the veggies with salt, pepper, Italian seasoning, ranch seasoning, and olive oil
3. Toss all the ingredients well.
4. Now divide this between two baskets of the air fryer.
5. Set zone 1 basket to AIRFRY mode at 360 degrees F for 25 minutes.
6. Select the Match button for the zone 2 basket.
7. Once it is cooked and done, serve, and enjoy.

Serving Suggestion: Serve it with rice

Variation Tip: None

Nutritional Information Per Serving: Calories 275| Fat 15.3g| Sodium129 mg | Carbs 33g | Fiber3.8 g | Sugar5 g | Protein 4.4g

Green Beans with Baked Potatoes

Prep: 15 Minutes | Cook Time: 45 Minutes | Makes: 2 Servings

Ingredients

- 2 cups of green beans
- 2 large potatoes, cubed
- 3 tablespoons of olive oil
- 1 teaspoon of seasoned salt
- ½ teaspoon chili powder
- 1/6 teaspoon garlic powder
- 1/4 teaspoon onion powder

Directions

1. Take a large bowl and pour olive oil into it.
2. Now add all the seasoning in the olive oil and whisk it well.
3. Toss the green bean in it, then transfer it to zone 1 basket of the air fryer.
4. Now season the potatoes with the seasoning and add them to the zone 2 basket.
5. Now set the zone one basket to AIRFRY mode at 350 degrees F for 18 minutes.
6. Now hit 2 for the second basket and set it to AIR FRY mode at 350 degrees F, for 45 minutes.
7. Once the cooking cycle is complete, take out and serve it by transferring it to the serving plates.

Serving Suggestion: serve with rice

Variation Tip: use canola oil instead of olive oil

Nutritional Information Per Serving: Calories473 | Fat21.6g | Sodium796 mg | Carbs 66.6g | Fiber12.9 g | Sugar6 g | Protein8.4 g

Cheesy Potatoes with Asparagus

Prep: 15 Minutes | Cook Time: 35 Minutes | Makes: 2 Servings

Ingredients

- 1-1/2 pounds of russet potato, wedges or cut in half
- 2 teaspoons mixed herbs
- 2 teaspoons chili flakes
- 2 cups asparagus
- 1 cup chopped onion
- 1 tablespoon Dijon mustard
- 1/4 cup fresh cream
- 1 teaspoon olive oil
- 2 tablespoons of butter
- 1/2 teaspoon salt and black pepper
- Water as required
- 1/2 cup Parmesan cheese

Directions

1. Take a bowl and add asparagus and sweet potato wedges to it.
2. Season it with salt, black pepper, and olive oil.
3. Now add the potato wedges to the zone 1 air fryer basket and asparagus to the zone 2 basket.
4. Set basket1 to AIRFRY mode at 390 degrees F for 12 minutes.
5. Set the zone 2 basket at 390 degrees F, for 30-35 minutes.
6. Meanwhile, take a skillet and add butter and sauté onion in it for a few minutes.
7. Then add salt and Dijon mustard and chili flakes, Parmesan cheese, and fresh cream.
8. Once the air fry mode is done, take out the potato and asparagus.
9. Drizzle the skillet ingredients over the potatoes and serve with asparagus.

Serving Suggestion: Serve with rice

Variation Tip: Use olive oil instead of butter

Nutritional Information Per Serving: Calories 251| Fat11g | Sodium 279mg | Carbs 31.1g | Fiber 5g | Sugar 4.1g | Protein9 g

Garlic Herbed Baked Potatoes

Prep: 25 Minutes | Cook Time: 45 Minutes | Makes: 4 Servings

Ingredients

- 4 large baking potatoes
- Salt and black pepper, to taste
- 2 teaspoons of avocado oil

Cheese ingredients

- 2 cups sour cream
- 1 teaspoon of garlic clove, minced
- 1 teaspoon fresh dill
- 2 teaspoons chopped chives
- Salt and black pepper, to taste
- 2 teaspoons Worcestershire sauce

Directions

1. Pierce the skin of potatoes with a fork.
2. Season the potatoes with olive oil, salt, and black pepper.
3. Divide the potatoes among two baskets of the ninja air fryer.
4. Now hit 1 for the first basket and set it to AIR FRY mode at 350 degrees F, for 45 minutes.
5. Select the MATCH button for zone 2.
6. Meanwhile, take a bowl and mix all the ingredient under cheese ingredients
7. Once the cooking cycle complete, take out and make a slit in-between the potatoes.
8. Add cheese mixture in the cavity and serve it hot.

Serving Suggestion: serve with gravy

Variation Tip: None

Nutritional Information Per Serving: Calories 382| Fat24.6 g| Sodium 107mg | Carbs 36.2g | Fiber 2.5g | Sugar2 g | Protein 7.3g

Kale and Spinach Chips

Prep: 12 Minutes | Cook Time: 6 Minutes | Makes: 2 Servings

Ingredients

- 2 cups spinach, torn in pieces and stem removed
- 2 cups kale, torn in pieces, stems removed
- 1 tablespoon of olive oil
- Sea salt, to taste
- 1/3 cup Parmesan cheese

Directions

1. Take a bowl and add spinach to it.
2. Take another bowl and add kale to it.
3. Now, season both of them with olive oil, and sea salt.
4. Add kale to zone 1 basket and spinach to zone 2 basket.
5. Select the zone 1 air fry mode at 350 degrees F for 6 minutes.
6. Set zone 2 to AIR FRY mode at 350 for 5 minutes.
7. Once done, take out the crispy chips and sprinkle Parmesan cheese on top.
8. Serve and Enjoy.

Serving Suggestion: Serve it with baked potato

Variation Tip: use canola oil instead of olive oil

Nutritional Information Per Serving: Calories 166| Fat 11.1g| Sodium 355mg | Carbs 8.1g | Fiber1.7 g | Sugar 0.1g | Protein 8.2g

Zucchini with Stuffing

Prep: 12 Minutes | Cook Time: 20 Minutes | Makes: 3 Servings

Ingredients

- 1 cup quinoa, rinsed
- 1 cup black olives
- 6 medium zucchinis, about 2 pounds
- 2 cups cannellini beans, drained
- 1 white onion, chopped
- ¼ cup almonds, chopped
- 4 cloves of garlic, chopped
- 4 tablespoons olive oil
- 1 cup of water
- 2 cups Parmesan cheese, for topping

Directions

1. First wash the zucchini and cut it lengthwise.
2. Take a skillet and heat oil in it
3. Sauté the onion in olive oil for a few minutes.
4. Then add the quinoa and water and let it cook for 8 minutes with the lid on the top.
5. Transfer the quinoa to a bowl and add all remaining ingredients excluding zucchini and Parmesan cheese.
6. Scoop out the seeds of zucchinis.
7. Fill the cavity of zucchinis with bowl mixture.
8. Top it with a handful of Parmesan cheese.
9. Arrange 4 zucchinis in both air fryer baskets.
10. Select zone1 basket at AIR FRY for 20 minutes and adjusting the temperature to 390 degrees F.
11. Use the Match button to select the same setting for zone 2.
12. Serve and enjoy.

Serving Suggestion: Serve it with pasta

Variation Tip: None

Nutritional Information Per Serving: Calories 1171| Fat 48.6g| Sodium 1747mg | Carbs 132.4g | Fiber 42.1g | Sugar 11.5g | Protein 65.7g

Brussels sprouts

Prep: 15 Minutes | Cook Time: 20 Minutes | Makes: 2 Servings

Ingredients

- 2 pounds Brussels sprouts
- 2 tablespoons avocado oil
- Salt and pepper, to taste
- 1 cup pine nuts, roasted

Directions

1. Trim the bottom of Brussels sprouts.
2. Take a bowl and combine the avocado oil, salt, and black pepper.
3. Toss the Brussels sprouts well.
4. Divide it in both air fryer baskets.
5. For the zone 1 basket use AIR fry mode for 20 minutes at 390 degrees F.
6. Select the MATCH button for the zone 2 basket.
7. Once the Brussels sprouts get crisp and tender, take out and serve.

Serving Suggestion: Serve with Rice

Variation Tip: Use olive oil instead of avocado oil

Nutritional Information Per Serving: Calories 672| Fat 50g| Sodium 115mg | Carbs 51g | Fiber 20.2g | Sugar 12.3g | Protein 25g

Stuffed Tomatoes

Prep: 12 Minutes | Cook Time: 8 Minutes | Makes: 2 Servings

Ingredients

- 2 cups brown rice, cooked
- 1 cup of tofu, grilled and chopped
- 4 large red tomatoes
- 4 tablespoons basil, chopped
- 1/4 tablespoon olive oil
- Salt and black pepper, to taste
- 2 tablespoons of lemon juice
- 1 teaspoon of red chili powder
- ½ cup Parmesan cheese

Directions

1. Take a large bowl and mix rice, tofu, basil, olive oil, salt, black pepper, lemon juice, and chili powder.
2. Take four large tomatoes and center core them.
3. Fill the cavity with the rice mixture.
4. Top it off with the cheese sprinkle.
5. Divide the tomatoes into two air fryer baskets.

6. turn on zone one basket and cook tomatoes at AIRFRY mode, for 8 minutes at 400 degrees F.
7. Select the MATCH button for zone two baskets, which cooks food by copying the setting across both zones.
8. Serve and enjoy.

Serving Suggestion: Serve it with Greek yogurt

Variation Tip: Use canola oil instead of olive oil.

Nutritional Information Per Serving: Calories 1034| Fat 24.2g| Sodium 527mg | Carbs165 g | Fiber12.1 g | Sugar 1.2g | Protein 43.9g

Chapter 8-Desserts Recipes

Cake in The Air Fryer

Prep: 12 Minutes | Cook Time: 30 Minutes | Makes: 2 Servings

Ingredients

- 90 grams all-purpose flour
- Pinch of salt
- 1/2 teaspoon of baking powder
- ½ cup of tutti fruitti mix
- 2 eggs
- 1 teaspoon of vanilla extract
- 10 tablespoons of white sugar

Directions

1. Take a bowl and add all-purpose flour, salt, and baking powder.
2. Stir it in a large bowl.
3. Whisk two eggs in a separate bowl and add vanilla extract, sugar and blend it with a hand beater.
4. Now combine wet ingredients with the dry ones.
5. Mix it well and pour it between two round pan that fits inside baskets.
6. Place the pans in both the baskets.
7. Now set the zone 1 basket to BAKE function at 310 for 30 minutes.
8. Select MATCH for zone two baskets.
9. Once it's done, serve and enjoy.

Serving Suggestion: Serve it with whipped cream

Variation Tip: Use brown sugar instead of white sugar

Nutritional Information Per Serving: Calories 711| Fat4.8g| Sodium 143mg | Carbs 161g | Fiber 1.3g | Sugar 105g | Protein 10.2g

Bread Pudding

Prep: 12 Minutes | Cook Time: 8-12 Minutes | Makes: 2 Servings

Ingredients

- Nonstick spray, for greasing ramekins
- 2 slices of white bread, crumbled
- 4 tablespoons of white sugar
- 5 large eggs
- ½ cup cream
- Salt, pinch
- 1/3 teaspoon of cinnamon powder

Directions

1. Take a bowl and whisk eggs in it.
2. Add sugar and salt to the egg and whisk it all well.
3. Then add cream and use a hand beater to incorporate the entire ingredients.
4. Now add cinnamon, and add crumbs of bread.
5. Mix it well and add into two round shaped baking pan.
6. Pace it in both zones of ninja air fryer.
7. Set it on AIRFRY mode at 350 degrees F for 8-12 minutes.
8. Press the MATCH button for zone 2.
9. Once it's cooked, serve.

Serving Suggestion: Serve it with Coffee

Variation Tip: Use brown sugar instead of white sugar

Nutritional Information Per Serving: Calories 331| Fat16.1g| Sodium 331mg | Carbs 31g | Fiber0.2g | Sugar 26.2g | Protein 16.2g

Mini Blueberry Pies

Prep: 12 Minutes | Cook Time: 10 Minutes | Makes: 2 Servings

Ingredients

- 1 box Store-Bought Pie Dough, Trader Joe's
- ¼ cup blueberry jam
- 1 teaspoon of lemon zest
- 1 egg white, for brushing

Directions

1. Take the store brought pie dough and cut it into 3-inch circles.
2. Brush the dough with egg white all around the parameters.
3. Now add blueberry jam and zest in the middle and top it with another circular.
4. Press the edges with the fork to seal it.
5. Make a slit in the middle of the dough and divide it between the baskets.
6. Set zone 1 to AIR FRY mode 360 degrees for 10 minutes.
7. Select the MATCH button for zone 2.
8. Once cooked, serve.

Serving Suggestion: Serve it with vanilla ice-cream

Variation Tip: use orange zest instead of lemon zest

Nutritional Information Per Serving: Calories 234| Fat8.6g| Sodium187 mg | Carbs 38.2 g | Fiber 0.1g | Sugar13.7 g | Protein 2g

Mini Strawberry and Cream Pies

Prep: 12 Minutes | Cook Time: 10 Minutes | Makes: 2 Servings

Ingredients

*   1 box Store-Bought Pie Dough, Trader Joe's
*   1 cup strawberries, cubed
*   3 tablespoons of cream, heavy
*   2 tablespoons of almonds
*   1 egg white, for brushing

Directions

1. Take the store brought pie dough and flatten it on a surface.
2. Use a round cutter to cut it into 3-inch circles.
3. Brush the dough with egg white all around the parameters.
4. Now add almonds, strawberries, and cream in a very little amount in the center of the dough, and top it with another circular.
5. Press the edges with the fork to seal it.
6. Make a slit in the middle of the dough and divide it into the baskets.
7. Set zone 1 to AIR FRY mode 360 degrees for 10 minutes.
8. Select MATCH for zone 2 basket.
9. Once done, serve.

Serving Suggestion: Serve it with vanilla ice-cream

Variation Tip: use orange zest instead of lemon zest

Nutritional Information Per Serving: Calories 203| Fat12.7g| Sodium 193mg | Carbs20 g | Fiber 2.2g | Sugar 5.8g | Protein 3.7g

Air Fryer Sweet Twists

Prep: 15 Minutes | Cook Time: 9 Minutes | Makes: 2 Servings

Ingredients

- 1 box store-bought puff pastry
- ½ teaspoon cinnamon
- ½ teaspoon sugar
- ½ teaspoon black sesame seeds
- Salt, pinch
- 2 tablespoons Parmesan cheese, freshly grated

Directions

1. Place the dough on a work surface.
2. Take a small bowl and mix cheese, sugar, salt, sesame seeds, and cinnamon.
3. Press this mixture on both sides of the dough.
4. Now, cut the pastry into 1" x 3" strips.
5. Twist each of the strips 2 times and then lay it onto the flat.
6. Transfer to both the air fryer baskets.
7. Select zone 1 to air fry mode at 400 degrees F for 9-10 minutes.
8. Select the MATCH button for the zone 2 basket.
9. Once cooked, serve.

Serving Suggestion: Serve it with champagne!

Variation Tip: None

Nutritional Information Per Serving: Calories 140| Fat9.4g| Sodium 142mg | Carbs 12.3g | Fiber0.8 g | Sugar 1.2g | Protein 2g

Chocolate Chip Muffins

Prep: 12 Minutes | Cook Time: 15 Minutes | Makes: 2 Servings

Ingredients

- Salt, pinch
- 2 eggs
- 1/3 cup brown sugar
- 1/3 cup butter
- 4 tablespoons of milk
- ¼ teaspoon of vanilla extract
- ½ teaspoon of baking powder
- 1 cup all-purpose flour
- 1 pouch chocolate chips, 35 grams

Directions

1. Take 4 oven-safe ramekins that are the size of a cup and layer them with muffin papers.
2. In a bowl, whisk the egg, brown sugar, butter, milk, and vanilla extract.
3. Whisk it all very well with an electric hand beater.
4. Now, in a second bowl, mix the flour, baking powder, and salt.
5. Now, mix the dry ingredients slowly into the wet ingredients.
6. Now, at the end fold in the chocolate chips and mix them well
7. Divide this batter into 4 ramekins.
8. Now, divide it between both zones.
9. Set the time for zone 1 to 15 minutes at 350 degrees F, at AIRFRY mode.
10. Select the MATCH button for the zone 2 basket.
11. Check if not done, and let it AIR FRY for one more minute.
12. Once it is done, serve.

Serving Suggestion: Serve it with chocolate syrup drizzle

Variation Tip: None

Nutritional Information Per Serving: Calories 757| Fat40.3g| Sodium 426mg | Carbs 85.4g | Fiber 2.2g | Sugar 30.4g | Protein 14.4g

Lemony Sweet Twists

Prep: 15 Minutes | Cook Time: 9 Minutes | Makes: 2 Servings

Ingredients

- 1 box store-bought puff pastry
- ½ teaspoon lemon zest
- 1 tablespoon of lemon juice
- 2 teaspoons brown sugar
- Salt, pinch
- 2 tablespoons Parmesan cheese, freshly grated

Directions

1. Put the puff pastry dough on a clean work area.
2. In a bowl, combine Parmesan cheese, brown sugar, salt, lemon zest, and lemon juice.
3. Press this mixture on both sides of the dough.
4. Now, cut the pastry into 1" x 4" strips.
5. Twist each of the strips.
6. Transfer to both the air fryer baskets.
7. Select zone 1 to air fry mode at 400 degrees F for 9-10 minutes.
8. Select match for zone 2 basket.
9. Once cooked, serve and enjoy.

Serving Suggestion: Serve it with champagne!

Variation Tip: None

Nutritional Information Per Serving: Calories 156| Fat10g| Sodium 215mg | Carbs 14g | Fiber 0.4g | Sugar3.3 g | Protein 2.8g

Chocolate Chip Cake

Prep: 12 Minutes | Cook Time: 15 Minutes | Makes: 4servings

Ingredients

- Salt, pinch
- 2 eggs, whisked
- ½ cup brown sugar
- ½ cup butter, melted
- 10 tablespoons of almond milk
- ¼ teaspoon of vanilla extract
- ½ teaspoon of baking powder
- 1 cup all-purpose flour
- 1 cup of chocolate chips
- ½ cup of cocoa powder

Directions

1. Take 2 round baking pan that fits inside the baskets of the air fryer.
2. layer it with baking paper, cut it to the size of a baking pan.
3. In a bowl, whisk the egg, brown sugar, butter, almond milk, and vanilla extract.
4. Whisk it all very well with an electric hand beater.
5. In a second bowl, mix the flour, cocoa powder, baking powder, and salt.
6. Now, mix the dry ingredients slowly with the wet ingredients.
7. Now, at the end fold in the chocolate chips.
8. Incorporate all the ingredients well.
9. Divide this batter into the round baking pan.
10. Set the time for zone 1 to 16 minutes at 350 degrees F at AIR FRY mode.
11. Select the MATCH button for the zone 2 baskets.
12. Check if not done, and let it AIR FRY for one more minute.
13. Once it is done, serve.

Serving Suggestion: Serve it with chocolate syrup drizzle

Variation Tip: Use baking soda instead of baking powder

Nutritional Information Per Serving: Calories 736| Fat45.5g| Sodium 356mg | Carbs 78.2g | Fiber 6.1g | Sugar 32.7g | Protein11.5 g

Pumpkin Muffins

Prep: 20 Minutes | Cook Time: 20 Minutes | Makes: 4 Servings

Ingredients

- 1 and ½ cups of all-purpose flour
- ½ teaspoon baking soda
- ½ teaspoon of baking powder
- 1 and 1/4 teaspoons cinnamon, groaned
- 1/4 teaspoon ground nutmeg, grated
- 2 large eggs
- Salt, pinch
- 3/4 cup granulated sugar
- 1/2 cup dark brown sugar
- 1 and 1/2 cups of pumpkin puree
- 1/4 cup coconut milk

Directions

1. Take 4 ramekins that are the size of a cup and layer them with muffin papers.
2. Crack an egg in a bowl and add brown sugar, baking soda, baking powder, cinnamon, nutmeg, and sugar.
3. Whisk it all very well with an electric hand beater.
4. Now, in a second bowl, mix the flour, and salt.
5. Now, mix the dry ingredients slowly with the wet ingredients.
6. Now, at the end fold in the pumpkin puree and milk, mix it well
7. Divide this batter into 4 ramekins.
8. Now, divide ramekins between both zones.
9. Set the time for zone 1 to 18 minutes at 360 degrees Fat AIRFRY mode.
10. Select the MATCH button for the zone 2 basket.
11. Check if not done, and let it AIR FRY for one more minute.
12. Once it is done, serve.

Serving Suggestion: Serve it with a glass of milk

Variation Tip: Use almond milk instead of coconut milk

Nutritional Information Per Serving: Calories 291| Fat6.4 g| Sodium 241mg | Carbs 57.1g | Fiber 4.4g | Sugar42 g | Protein 5.9g

Fudge Brownies

Prep: 20 Minutes | Cook Time: 16 Minutes | Makes: 4 Servings
Ingredients

- 1/2 cup all-purpose flour
- 1/4 cup unsweetened cocoa powder
- 3/4 teaspoon kosher salt
- 2 large eggs, whisked
- 1 tablespoon almond milk
- 1/2 cup brown sugar
- 1/2 cup packed white sugar
- 1/2 tablespoon vanilla extract
- 8 ounces of semisweet chocolate chips, melted
- 2/4 cup unsalted butter, melted

Directions

1. Take a medium bowl, and use a hand beater to whisk together eggs, milk, both the sugars and vanilla.
2. In a separate microwave-safe bowl, mix melted butter and chocolate and microwave it for 30 seconds to melt the chocolate.
3. Add all the listed dry ingredients to the chocolate mixture.
4. Now incorporate the egg bowl ingredient into the batter.
5. Spray a reasonable size round baking pan that fits in baskets of air fryer
6. Grease the pan with cooking spray.
7. Now pour the batter into the pan, put the crisper plate in baskets.
8. Add the pans and insert the basket into the unit.
9. Select the AIR FRY mode and adjust the setting the temperature to 300 degrees F, for 30 minutes.
10. Check it after 35 minutes and if not done, cook for 10 more minutes
11. Once it's done, take it out and let it get cool before serving.
12. Enjoy.

Serving Suggestion: Serve it with a dollar of the vanilla ice cream
Variation Tip: Use dairy milk instead of almond milk
Nutritional Information Per Serving: Calories 760| Fat43.3 g| Sodium644 mg | Carbs 93.2g | Fiber5.3 g | Sugar 70.2g | Protein 6.2g

Chapter 9-3 Weeks Diet Plan

Days	Breakfast	Lunch	Dinner
Day1	BREAKFAST SAUSAGE OMELET &SWEET BITES	CHICKEN THIGHS WITH BRUSSELS SPROUTS & CHEDDAR QUICHE	FISH AND CHIPS & KALE AND SPINACH CHIPS
Day 2	YELLOW POTATOES WITH EGGS & STRAWBERRIES AND WALNUTS MUFFINS	CHICKEN & BROCCOLI & BRUSSELS SPROUTS	SPICE-RUBBED CHICKEN PIECES & MIXED AIR FRY VEGGIES
Day 3	EGG WITH BABY SPINACH&GRILL CHEESE SANDWICH	SPICY CHICKEN &KALE AND SPINACH CHIPS	BEER BATTERED FISH FILLET & CHEESY POTATOES WITH ASPARAGUS
Day 4	SWEET POTATOES HASH& DIJON CHEESE SANDWICH	SPICY FISH FILLET WITH ONION RINGS &BRUSSELS SPROUTS	FROZEN BREADED FISH FILLET & MIXED AIR FRY VEGGIES
Day 5	BANANA AND RAISINS MUFFINS& GRILL CHEESE SANDWICH	CHICKEN & BROCCOLI & SALMON WITH GREEN BEANS	BEEF & BROCCOLI & STUFFED TOMATOES
Day 6	EGG WITH BABY	TWO-WAY SALMON &	YUMMY CHICKEN BREASTS &STUFFED TOMATOES

	SPINACH&GRILL CHEESE SANDWICH	SPICED CHICKEN AND VEGETABLES	
Day 7	SWEET POTATOES HASH &DIJON CHEESE SANDWICH	CHICKEN BREAST STRIPS &Keto Baked Salmon With Pesto	STEAK AND MASHED CREAMY POTATOES & ZUCCHINI WITH STUFFING
Day 8	YELLOW POTATOES WITH EGGS &BLUEBERRIES MUFFINS	WINGS WITH CORN ON COB & BRUSSELS SPROUTS	CHICKEN LEG PIECE &STUFFED TOMATOES
Day 9	EGG AND AVOCADO IN THE NINJA FOODI &DIJON CHEESE SANDWICH	SPICE-RUBBED CHICKEN PIECES & BRUSSELS SPROUTS	CHINESE BBQ PORK & CHEESY POTATOES WITH ASPARAGUS
Day 10	BACON AND EGG OMELET &BLUEBERRIES MUFFINS	SPICY FISH FILLET WITH ONION RINGS	SHORT RIBS & ROOT VEGETABLES
Day 11	EGG WITH BABY SPINACH &BLUEBERRIES MUFFINS	FISH AND CHIPS & BRUSSELS SPROUTS	PORK CHOPS & FRESH MIX VEGGIES IN AIR FRYER
Day 12	YELLOW POTATOES WITH EGGS&GRILL	CHICKEN & BROCCOLI & STUFFED TOMATOES	GLAZED STEAK RECIPE &ZUCCHINI WITH STUFFING

	CHEESE SANDWICH		
Day 13	SWEET POTATOES HASH &GRILL CHEESE SANDWICH	WINGS WITH CORN ON COB & ZUCCHINI WITH STUFFING	STEAK IN AIR FRY & GARLIC HERBED BAKED POTATOES
Day 14	EGG AND AVOCADO IN THE NINJA FOODI & BLUEBERRIES MUFFINS	GLAZED THIGHS WITH FRENCH FRIES &BRUSSELS SPROUTS	YOGURT LAMB CHOPS & CHEESY POTATOES WITH ASPARAGUS
Day 15	BANANA AND RAISINS MUFFINS &DIJON CHEESE SANDWICH	GLAZED THIGHS WITH FRENCH FRIES	HAM BURGER PATTIES & GARLIC HERBED BAKED POTATOES
Day 16	BACON AND EGG OMELET & DIJON CHEESE SANDWICH	CHEDDAR QUICHE & GARLIC HERBED BAKED POTATOES	FROZEN BREADED FISH FILLET & Garlic Potato Wedges In Air Fryer
Day 17	BACON AND EGGS FOR BREAKFAST &BLUEBERRIES MUFFINS	CHICKEN WINGS & Garlic Potato Wedges In Air Fryer	SPICY LAMB CHOPS & STUFFED TOMATOES
Day 18	SAUSAGE WITH EGGS	BELL PEPPERS WITH SAUSAGES	BEEF RIBS &

	&GRILL CHEESE SANDWICH	&GREEN BEANS WITH BAKED POTATOES	GARLIC HERBED BAKED POTATOES
Day 19	BREAKFAST SAUSAGE OMELET &BLUEBERRIES MUFFINS	BEEF RIBS & GREEN BEANS WITH BAKED POTATOES	BELL PEPPERS WITH SAUSAGES & STUFFED TOMATOES
Day 20	BACON AND EGG OMELET & BLUEBERRIES MUFFINS	GLAZED THIGHS WITH FRENCH FRIES & STUFFED TOMATOES	SPICY LAMB CHOPS & FRESH MIX VEGGIES IN AIR FRYER
Day 21	BREAKFAST CASSEROLE &GRILL CHEESE SANDWICH	CHEDDAR QUICHE & GARLIC HERBED BAKED POTATOES	HAM BURGER PATTIES &STUFFED TOMATOES

Conclusion

All the MYTHS have gone, as this cookbook help, you prepared a wide variety of meals using an air fryer.

No doubt once you buy this appliance you will surely be impressed by its usefulness and wide cooking functionality.

Moreover, this cookbook is written in a very exciting yet easy tone, so that as a beginner you can prepare some delicious homemade recipes

The recipe collection is versatile and packed with flavor and nutrition. The ingredients are not expensive and are available at the local stores. Hopefully, in the end, the users can fulfill their aim of creating new recipes using an air fryer, as it improves the overall experience of cooking because of its preset button and quick heating technology.

The recipes prepare in an air fryer are loaded with nutrition and are less in fat. We highly recommend buying it for you.